Alternatives to the Peace Corps

Alternatives to the Peace Corps

A Directory of Global Volunteer Opportunities

TENTH EDITION

Edited by Jennifer Sage Willsea

FOOD FIRST BOOKS
Oakland, California

Cover design: Judy Hicks / Hicks Studio
Interior design: Jeff Brandenburg / Image-Comp.com
Cover photo: Peter Rosset

Tenth edition, 2003

Food First Books
398 60th Street
Oakland, California 94618
www.foodfirst.org

ISBN 0–935028–91–9

Food First Books are distributed by:
Client Distribution Services
425 Madison Avenue, Suite 1500
New York, NY 10017
(800) 343-4499

Printed in Canada

10 9 8 7 6 5 4 3 2 1

Contents

Acknowledgments

Alternatives to the Peace Corps has been developed in response to the numerous inquiries Food First receives from individuals seeking opportunities to gain community development experience.

Becky Buell, a staff member at Food First from 1985 to 1988, researched and wrote the original edition in 1986, with the assistance of Kari Hamerschlag, a Food First intern. Tremendous demand for the original book created a continuing need to revise and update it periodically.

Jennifer Sage Willsea revised the introduction and updated and expanded the listings of volunteer opportunities for this tenth edition, with help from Meaghan Reule and Clancy Drake.

This book is made possible by the organizations, volunteers, and friends who provide updates and additions each year. Many thanks go to the returned Peace Corps volunteers who have offered their perspectives in the development of this guide.

Preface

The "worldwide web" is an apt description of more than just our Internet connections. Overall, the diverse peoples and nations of the world are becoming more and more mutually dependent. International volunteering is one of the more positive aspects of the globalization of our economies, cultures, and social and political structures. The more negative side of globalization emerges in trade pacts and common markets and through the consolidation of capital by a handful of multinational corporations, while the gap between rich and poor continues to increase. Volunteering is widely viewed as a way to support more broad-based development and promote social justice in troubled areas of the world, and the number, stature, and influence of volunteer-based organizations has increased markedly over recent decades. Under the auspices of numerous government agencies and nongovernmental organizations (NGOs), countless individuals have volunteered their time and resources to bring about social change.

The Cold War ushered in a special kind of international development aid that was part of a battle for the minds and loyalties of emerging nations. Established by President Kennedy in 1961, the Peace Corps was intended to serve as a public relations tool to counter Soviet influence and, indeed, it was perceived as a form of benevolent foreign aid with a young American face. Tens of thousands of Americans have worked abroad through the Peace Corps since then, bringing home valuable experiences of foreign countries and the inner workings of government-sponsored aid. On the other hand, as we shall see in the next section, the Peace Corps has been strongly criticized for a number of reasons.

Since the Kennedy era, two generations of Americans have grown up supporting civil rights at home and seeking change in American foreign policy toward Vietnam, El Salvador, Nicaragua, South Africa, the Middle East, and a host of other regions. Many believe that US foreign policy has not always been helpful in building more equitable societies in developing nations. Neither human rights nor sustainable development has been the first priority of government foreign aid.

At Food First, we have researched world hunger extensively. Our analyses have led us to conclude that hunger is not caused by scarcity of food, or poor people's lack of know-how, or even overpopulation; it is caused by an unequal system of food production and distribution that enriches a small segment of society. Because of these inequalities, we emphasize the role of volunteers as participants in social change that is designed by and for local people.

Food First published the first edition of *Alternatives to the Peace Corps* in 1986 as a response to frequent requests for guidance on international volunteer opportunities that had no or minimal government strings attached. *Alternatives to the Peace Corps* was the first guide of its kind that offered options for voluntary service with private agencies that emphasized social change. The organizations and programs listed here seek volunteers who are willing to learn about local culture and support efforts by local grassroots organizations.

Another important priority in publishing *Alternatives to the Peace Corps* is to help place volunteers with agencies working for social and political reform in the United States. Hunger and poverty are not just foreign problems; here at home one in five children are growing up in poverty. The gap between rich and poor is increasing, creating a large underclass. Americans have always had a tradition of volunteer work; volunteerism has supported many of our community-based organizations, from parent-school groups and the YMCA/YWCA to coalitions against homelessness. Dedicated volunteers for self-help initiatives are needed more than ever today to counteract government cuts in programs for the disadvantaged, the elderly, immigrants, and the poor.

This tenth edition of *Alternatives to the Peace Corps* is dedicated to the men and women, young and old, who want to share their talents with humanity to make this a better world.

PART I

Alternatives to the
Peace Corps

Moving Beyond the Peace Corps

Deciding to volunteer is difficult. Knowing why you want to volunteer is the first step toward choosing from among a huge variety of options: where to go, with what organization, and with what funds. A common solution to this dilemma is to choose a government-sponsored volunteer program, such as the Peace Corps of the United States, in which all expenses are paid, and training, health and accident insurance, travel expenses, and even a stipend are provided. Serving with a government agency may also seem inherently safer than traveling thousands of miles from home under the auspices of a tiny nongovernmental organization (NGO) working for social change. The Peace Corps name commands a level of recognition and respect that less well-known groups are hard-pressed to match.

This solution seems simple enough. But the Peace Corps and programs like it are not always as straightforward as they seem. The countries in which an agency works, the projects it supports, and the role of its volunteers have many political, social, and cultural implications. Volunteers are more than well-meaning individuals. They are representatives of the governmental, religious, or institutional values and objectives of the organization that sponsors them.

For example, the Peace Corps is an agency of the US government. The Peace Corps volunteer is part of the national team dispatched by the US State Department and is accountable to the US ambassador in the host country. The Peace Corps is inevitably linked to US foreign policy objectives, as is the Peace Corps volunteer.

The Peace Corps was founded by President John F. Kennedy to build America's positive image at home and overseas during the Cold

War. In his 1961 inaugural address, Kennedy challenged young Americans to join "a grand and global alliance . . . to fight tyranny, poverty, disease, and war. . . ." The Peace Corps was ostensibly an apolitical organization, but its image was tainted from the outset by underlying foreign policy agendas. One initial goal of the Peace Corps was to counter Soviet cultural and political influence in developing nations; it was one tool used by the administration to eliminate the perceived threat of communism and to promote capitalism abroad.

The role of the Peace Corps in this agenda of the US government was no secret in its early years. A 1962 National Security Action Memorandum signed by Kennedy ordered the directors of the CIA, the United States Agency for International Development (USAID), and the Peace Corps to "give utmost attention and emphasis to programs designed to counter Communist indirect aggression [through] . . . support of local police forces for internal security and counterinsurgency purposes." Because the Peace Corps was closely linked to the CIA during its first decade, it lost credibility in some countries.

Prodded by a Senate committee investigating intelligence agencies in 1977, the CIA reported that it had not used the Peace Corps as a cover for its operations since 1975. The assertion may have been intended as reassurance, but it raises concerns about what those operations were and whether they continue today under a different dispensation. In 2003, the Russian government ended an eleven-year contract with the Peace Corps, accusing Peace Corps volunteers of attempting to gather information about Russian officials. Although these accusations were dismissed by the Peace Corps, they arise in the context of a history of questionable Peace Corps connections to the CIA and of touchy relations between the US and Russia. As we will explore further, the Peace Corps still has strong ties to the US government's foreign policy interests and is far from an apolitical organization.

The ideological underpinnings of the Peace Corps have altered to reflect the changing nature and objectives of US foreign policy over time. By the 1990s, US foreign policy was no longer defined primarily by the military influence of the Cold War but by its ability to mold societies through economic intervention. By influencing the patterns of resource control, legislation, and monetary policy within developing countries, whether through the International Monetary Fund (IMF) and World Bank's imposed structural adjustment programs or through free trade policies implemented by the World Trade Organization (WTO) and the North American Free Trade Agreement (NAFTA), the US government has found new ways to keep developing nations safe for its brand of capitalism.

The Peace Corps reflected this shift beginning in the 1980s. Under the leadership of director Loret Miller Ruppe during the Reagan administration, the Peace Corps began billing itself less as a symbol of goodwill and more seriously as a so-called development agency. Through initiatives such as the African Food System Initiative and the Competitive Enterprise Development Program, Peace Corps volunteers began promoting private enterprise and the development of export production in the rural sector.

The development of these programs coincided with economic policies handed down from the IMF and World Bank, which have pushed poor farmers away from growing basic food crops and toward planting specialty crops for foreign markets. This is economically risky and environmentally unsound and often results in farmers falling irretrievably into debt as they start planting for export, eventually losing their land. Many impoverished countries now import basic grains and legumes that were available locally and in great variety before. The net impact of these changes has eroded the standing of poor farmers and has contributed to the spread of hunger. Peace Corps volunteers in some countries abetted this agricultural shift despite their benevolent intentions.

This example of agricultural development points to a recurring theme in the history of the Peace Corps. While the stated goals of the Peace Corps and the intentions of Peace Corps volunteers are for the betterment of the world community, they are consistently undermined by US policies that perpetuate economic disparities and human rights abuses, as well as hinder development for poor communities. Former president John F. Kennedy established the Peace Corps "to promote world peace and friendship." While Peace Corps volunteers are stationed across six continents, the US government leads the world in weapons sales and military training (to countries including Colombia, the Philippines, Pakistan, and Uzbekistan) and is one of the major advocates of IMF and World Bank structural adjustment programs. These policies promote neither peace or friendship with the people of developing nations, and as an instrument of US policy, the Peace Corps cannot escape being tainted by them.

Another example of well-intended Peace Corps projects coinciding with damaging US policies is the role volunteers often take as teachers. Peace Corps volunteers are assigned to teach a wide array of subjects in developing nations, from math to HIV/AIDS awareness. While these volunteers are devoting their time and energy to education, however, other US policies harm the education systems in the very same countries. US-backed IMF and World Bank structural adjustment programs (required for nations to renegotiate their foreign debt) often require the governments of these nations to cut education budgets. US taxpayers pay about $80,000 for the training and service of each Peace Corps volunteer. That amount of money could pay the salaries of forty or more local teachers in many of the countries where the Peace Corps runs programs.

The argument is often made that the Peace Corps simply goes where it is invited and does what it is asked to do. That's true, up to a point. But the projects the agency is willing to engage in and the numbers of volunteers it is willing to send—both with an eye to geopolitical interest—also enter into the equation. Foreign governments, not grassroots organizations, submit the requests for volunteers, and there is no guarantee that they have their citizens' best interests at heart.

US foreign policy and the US government's goals for the Peace Corps took a new turn following the events of September 11, 2001. In an effort to counter anti-American sentiment around the globe and particularly in the Middle East, President George W. Bush called for Americans to make a renewed commitment to volunteerism. In his 2002 State of the Union address, Bush unveiled the USA Freedom Corps, an umbrella organization to include the Peace Corps, AmeriCorps, and the Senior Corps, as well as a new Citizens Corps, whose purpose is to focus on the prevention of and emergency response to terrorism. President Bush called for the Peace Corps to double in size by 2007 and to expand its mission "to go into the Islamic world to spread the message of economic development and really share the compassion of a great nation." Thus the Peace Corps' mission has become repoliticized as part of the post-9/11 War on Terrorism: the Peace Corps is cited by the Bush administration as a tool in the fight to "overcome evil." In fact, Bush frequently blends his messages about terrorism with a call to public service. Although increased volunteerism is a noble request at a time when the world needs people working for positive change, the president's motives are made questionable by the fact that his calls for American service across the globe are accompanied by the dismantling and defunding of a myriad of social programs in the US and abroad, from sex education to affordable health care. Moreover, the Bush administration has not followed through with its promised support to volunteer programs. Congress appropriated only about $25 million of the initially promised $230 million for Freedom Corps programs in 2003.

One Peace Corps volunteer's response to the new Freedom Corps illuminates some of these contradictions. This volunteer, serving in the Ivory Coast, criticized Bush's proposal to double the size of the Peace Corps because "it wouldn't do much to alleviate the poverty and hopelessness that foster terrorism. For, in reality, the Peace Corps does more to make us Americans feel good about ourselves than it does to fight poverty. Instead, we need to change the economic policies that I often find are punishing the very villagers I am trying to help." He cited the farm subsidy bill signed by Bush in May 2002, which increased subsidies to US cotton growers while African cotton farmers have to sell their cotton in a market depressed partly by overproduction in the US. "Expanding the Peace Corps is a nice gesture. But if that's the sort of carrot we're using alongside the very big stick of US economic and military might, it isn't much of a meal. . . . What we really need to do is fill the stomachs and pocketbooks of the developing world."

Structural Adjustment

During the 1980s and 1990s international agencies such as the IMF and the World Bank forced structural changes on economies in the developing world. Loans desperately needed to restructure foreign debts were conditioned on the performance of "structural adjustment" programs, technocratic plans whose declared aim was to make economies more "efficient," "competitive," and capable of growth. In fact, a principal effect, and perhaps even aim, of these programs has been to pry open the economies of developing nations for foreign corporations, providing new markets and investment opportunities. This has been accomplished by imposing diverse free-market policies, including privatization of state enterprises, deregulation (removal of restrictions on investment, both domestic and foreign), slashing of government budgets for health, education, and social services, and removal of import barriers. In country after country, the impact of these adjustments on the living conditions of the majority has been disastrous. Carried out on a large scale and in a very short time span, privatization transferred the benefits of institutions and resources from the general public to private businesses. In most countries, the gap between rich and poor widened as economic power became more sharply concentrated in increasingly fewer hands. As a result, poverty and hunger escalated in the developing world during the 1980s and early 1990s, especially in Latin America and Africa, where "adjustment" was more assiduously implemented by local elites. The IMF and World Bank continue to loan conditionally to developing nations. However, the IMF no longer refers to these as "structural adjustment" policies. In 1999, the IMF replaced the Enhanced Structural Adjustment Facility with the Poverty Reduction and Growth Facility, although the function is essentially the same.

(Source: *World Hunger: Twelve Myths,* by Frances Moore Lappé, Joseph Collins, and Peter Rosset, 1999, p. 103.)

If the Peace Corps is serious about its goal of capacity building (in development lingo, imparting skills and knowledge rather than simply performing charity), then it may assist host nations right out of their need for the Peace Corps. This should not be considered a bad thing.

Volunteering for the Peace Corps

Many Peace Corps volunteers would argue that their placement had little or nothing to do with the larger policy objectives of the US government. One volunteer working in a mountain region of the Philippines had no contact with the Peace Corps office, USAID, or any other Peace Corps volunteer in his two years of service. "I arrived at the community and worked out my role with them," he explained. Most volunteers believe that their service had a positive impact, independent of the other agencies and policy initiatives of the US government. "I worked with women to develop composting techniques and planting vegetables," said a volunteer working in Honduras. "These are techniques that will benefit them for a lifetime."

Despite the fact that some Peace Corps volunteers have felt their work was autonomous from US government policy, the link is inherent, and federal lawmakers have referred to the connection as a matter of course. "If there is a person in the Peace Corps who feels he cannot support US foreign policy, then he ought not to be in the Peace Corps," stated Senator Ross Adair (R-Ind). Loret Miller Ruppe, director of the Peace Corps for eight years, proclaimed proudly at the outset of her tenure in 1981 that she hoped to prove her agency's work "a valuable source of real aid to US foreign policy."

In general, the Peace Corps discourages expressions of dissent from federal doctrine. During the Vietnam War, the Peace Corps stipulated that no public disapproval of the war would be tolerated, and in a widely publicized incident, a volunteer in Chile was dismissed after he wrote a letter denouncing the war to a Chilean newspaper. Yet even keeping one's views silent and working diligently to encourage real development may not be a sufficient shield from policy imperatives. A pair of volunteers in Honduras in the 1980s were commanded to "name the names" of local citizens that their sector boss believed were communists. Prospective volunteers should think carefully about how their political views may be inhibited by their placement with the Peace Corps.

Other criticisms have been leveled at the Peace Corps over the years. Former volunteers and staff have accused the agency of providing insufficient training, of defining goals and tasks too vaguely, and of withholding follow-through, thus hindering the long-term sustainability of projects. Returnees note that the Peace Corps often uses the presence or number of volunteers sent as a bargaining chip in its relations with other countries. During the 1980s, Central American nations allied with the US were flooded with volunteers to counterbalance the heightened US military presence there and to put a good face on the intervention against Sandinista Nicaragua.

Despite all the concerns about the Peace Corps as an arm of US foreign policy, the agency must be credited with enabling thousands of American citizens to witness the realities of poverty and injustice in developing nations. The refrain one hears over and over again in statements from returned volunteers is "I got much more than I gave." Most Peace Corps volunteers will attest that living and working alongside people in poor communities was the most powerful experience of their lives, one which has influenced their decisions and actions ever since. Many returned Peace Corps volunteers have learned through their placement about the intimate connections between development and economic justice, militarization and human rights. They return to the US and work to make US foreign and domestic policy more accountable to the poor.

As one returned Peace Corps volunteer explained, "If there is one thing to thank the Peace Corps for, it's for showing me how US policies hurt the average person. In a country like Paraguay, it is hard to miss the connection between US aid and the oppression of the poor. It is hard to miss the links between the IMF economic package and the inability of the poor to feed themselves. These realizations radically changed my perspectives on the world." But the Peace Corps is not the only way to have such valuable experiences.

United States Agency for International Development

A look at some of the other federal agencies involved in development work is in order. The US Agency for International Development (USAID), created by Kennedy in 1961, the same year as the Peace Corps, states frankly on its website that the purpose of US aid to other nations is to further America's foreign policy interests. Through field offices in foreign countries, USAID funnels monetary aid and technical assistance to projects in keeping with the purposes of foreign policy. Some of these projects have involved leaning on governments to privatize state-owned industries, allow greater foreign investment, and decrease spending on social programs such as health, education, and food subsidies. USAID has helped to uphold the regime of debt service imposed upon many poor countries by the IMF and the World Bank and to enforce the claims of US corporations conducting business abroad. Too often, the agency has pushed for costly solutions to local problems, and its projects have enriched only the wealthiest citizens of developing nations. In this guide, we have tried to avoid listing organizations that accept money from USAID.

VISTA and AmeriCorps

The government volunteer service program in the US, now known as AmeriCorps, offers another interesting comparison to the Peace Corps. In 1964, President Johnson created VISTA (Volunteers in Service to America) as the "domestic Peace Corps," and in 1993 under President Clinton, VISTA was replaced by the Corporation for National Service, or AmeriCorps. The purpose of both of these programs was and is to address issues such as homelessness, illiteracy, and economic and neighborhood revitalization through placements with nonprofits, public agencies, and faith-based organizations. As with the Peace Corps, volunteers are prohibited from engaging in political activity during their participation, and there can be little doubt that the stated aims of the projects AmeriCorps (and VISTA before it) supports seldom run counter to official US policy on poverty. Yet, in its early years, VISTA's emphasis on community organizing and self-help over service delivery—as well as its removal from the realm of foreign relations and the imperative of upholding our image overseas—garnered the agency a reputation for activism, even radicalism. VISTA later assisted with the implementation of and support for welfare reform legislation, which undermined its goal of reducing poverty. Over the years, VISTA gradually shifted its focus away from remedying poverty and toward more general service endeavors; it promoted volunteerism less as an agent of social change and more as a salutary and fulfilling activity for concerned citizens. Like USAID and the Peace Corps, its first concern is the proper placement and use of the aid giver, not the long-term needs of the aid receiver.

President Bush realigned AmeriCorps with domestic and foreign federal policies in 2002, when he asked for the expansion of AmeriCorps to assist with homeland security and the War on Terrorism. The Citizens Service Act that described this expansion also included changes to the pledge taken by AmeriCorps volunteers. Previously the pledge focused on community service, made no mention of the US Constitution, and had no religious references. In this bill, however, officials proposed a new pledge in which volunteers would promise to support the Constitution of the United States "in God's name." This pledge would be voluntary, but clearly there is a push in Washington for increased political and religious influence on AmeriCorps public service programs.

AmeriCorps, like the Peace Corps, is inherently infused with the American government's agenda, and since September 11, 2001, this relationship has intensified. Whether or not one regards this melding of American service with government policies as questionable, the administration's stated commitment to increased volunteerism was not backed up with the necessary funds. President Bush repeatedly praised AmeriCorps in his calls to American volunteerism and proposed a 50 percent increase in its size. However, congressional funding was dramatically reduced for 2003, and AmeriCorps will be able to support only 35,000 workers in 2003, a 30 percent reduction from 2002. This leaves countless organizations without volunteers and thus unable to fulfill the social services their communities need.

Nongovernmental Organizations

Much has been said and written over the last two decades about the proliferation of nongovernmental organizations throughout the world and their potential for enacting social and political change. In countries of the developing and developed world—of the global South and the global North—the last twenty years have witnessed a massive upsurge in the number of citizens' organizations airing grievances, lobbying for redress, mobilizing protests, establishing needed services for their constituents, and advocating for democratization of the forces of market and state. Concurrent has been the rise of resource or support organizations, often but not exclusively in the North, that provide research, advice, information, grants, or other aid to citizens' groups or to broader movements. In the North, both kinds of groups are generally referred to as NGOs, "civil society," or the "voluntary sector" or "third sector" (as in a sector separate from both the market and the state); in the US, NGOs are often called "nonprofits." Many in the global South distinguish between NGOs, which offer research and support, and civil society groups or social movements, which have a popular base. Lester Salamon, director of the Institute for Policy Studies at Johns Hopkins University, has used the term "associational revolution" to describe the growing size and strength of civil society groups of all kinds. Their appeal to believers throughout the political spectrum is considerable, and their successes have inspired much optimism that they can accomplish what market and state have failed to bring about. To name just one example, concerted networking among hundreds of civil society organizations put thousands of protesters on the streets of Seattle during the WTO's Third Ministerial Conference in 1999, the start of a growing global movement for economic and social justice, manifested in the streets of cities all over the world in the last few years.

However, the emphasis on third sector solutions can conceal a retreat from necessary government-supported solutions to poverty and injustice, such as agrarian reform or income redistribution. In the present day, when fifty-one of the hundred largest economies in the world are transnational corporations, one cannot be too complacent about the strength of the market or the role governments play in enforcing inequalities of wealth. The presence of the third sector in and of itself is not a cure for social problems. It is a powerful tool, but one tool among several.

Nevertheless, the future of nongovernmental organizations and social movements appears promising. These days USAID and the Peace Corps employ the rhetoric of "grassroots empowerment" and "local decision-making" in describing their own projects. We welcome this sign of the trickling up of NGO influence and can only hope that there is sufficient substance behind the words to make a real difference in some people's lives.

The organizations in this book are, or work in cooperation with, NGOs and citizens' groups—not the government—in countries receiving volunteers. International cooperation among these groups is no guarantee against wasted or misguided efforts, but at least the work that gets accomplished is much less likely to be confused with or compromised by the agendas of government, either ours or someone else's. Readers of this book are encouraged to involve themselves in truly sustainable development. We can build international cooperation most effectively through the empowerment and leadership of local people.

Assessing Your Needs and Narrowing Your Search

Choosing a volunteer program involves assessing your own ideals and personal needs and then finding an organization or program that matches those best. You may know that you want to work with children or on sustainable development, or that you want to work with an organization that is completely run by local people rather than one that is based in the US or Europe. You may have only a month to volunteer or financial constraints that affect the type of program you are able to do, or its location. In order to match your needs it is important to be informed of the different possibilities and their strengths and weaknesses.

What Sorts of Projects Are Available?

In a few pages, we'll get to assessing your own needs and options and evaluating organizations. First, though, let's take a look at the types of opportunities that are available, and what their benefits and drawbacks might be.

Long-Term Projects

The Peace Corps requires a two-year commitment from its volunteers, and this is not without good reason. Whether you are planning to volunteer in Zimbabwe or in Arizona, the more time you spend there, the better you will understand the community and the more you will be able to contribute. Particularly in the first months of your volunteer experience, you will mostly be learning from the people you are working with, and it takes a long time before you develop the knowledge and connections necessary to even begin to effect change. Drawbacks of this kind of commitment are obvious—a long-term, intensive experience is not for everyone. You may have other financial or time commitments, or family responsibilities, that keep you from taking on a volunteer stint of a year or more. And, if you are not going through an organization that offers a living stipend, you may worry about how you can support yourself as a volunteer for such a long time. If this is the case, read the section on fundraising in this chapter—it has some suggestions for making a long-term volunteer commitment financially possible.

Short-Term Opportunities

While some organizations require a minimum six-month or one-year commitment from volunteers —and this is the best way to learn and contribute most effectively and deeply— you may not have the freedom to spend more than a month volunteering. Some of the organizations listed in the International and US sections of this book run shorter programs that focus on cultural exchange as well as service projects to benefit the community you are visiting. Be aware that a shorter-term commitment will probably end up being more of a cultural exchange, and an excellent educational experience for you, than a chance to see a substantial service project through. However, a well-run program offering shorter-term volunteer slots can still be of genuine service to a local community.

Alternative Travel

If your time is limited, you may also want to look into socially responsible trips and tours. Several organizations and travel agencies lead "reality tours" abroad. These are socially responsible educational tours that provide participants with firsthand experience of the political, economic, and social structures that create or promote hunger, poverty, and environmental degradation. Tours offer an opportunity to meet people with diverse perspectives on agriculture, development, and the environment. They often include the opportunity to stay with local people, visit rural areas, and meet with grassroots organizers.

Such tours can alter your understanding of hunger and poverty and direct you to areas where you can best work for democratic social change. These are great opportunities for people who need a shorter-term, intensive, and well-structured experience. However, these are not always the cheapest option and are usually more educational than service-oriented.

Volunteering as a Student

A number of universities offer study abroad programs that provide an opportunity to learn about the political, economic, and social conditions in a given country; several of these programs are listed in the Alternative Travel and Study Overseas section of this book. It is possible, however, to combine almost any sort of overseas study program with volunteer work, if you are enterprising. Once established in a country, seek out individuals and groups directly involved with community development. They may be able to direct you to an appropriate volunteer placement where you can build your skills and experience in the field. Working in this way can give you the contacts, experience, and confidence you may need for a longer or more intensive overseas experience when you are finished with school.

Professional/Skilled Exchange

Many organizations welcome volunteers with specific technical skills in such fields as construction, health care, and agriculture. If you have some years of experience in a particular area, working directly with an organization or community that needs people with your experience is a great opportunity for you. Organizations geared less toward accommodating American volunteers and more focused on local, grassroots work will often only accept volunteers with very specific skills that the organization is lacking and needs to further their work. This kind of volunteer opportunity is probably one of the best ways to do truly effective work for a community. The closer your skills match their needs, and the more involved you can be on a practical level, the more productive your experience will be for both you and the community you are working in. In any work experience, local people can best define your role. Let them know what your skills are and allow them to decide how they can best put those skills to use.

Working Overseas

Most overseas development positions require two or more years of community development experience. While a two-year volunteer post does not guarantee future employment, you may find that by developing your skills and connections with communities in the developing world, job possibilities will open up. To guide you in your job search, you will find organizations and publications in the Resources section that list employment openings overseas.

Designing Your Own Experience

For someone who has significant travel experience and a solid focus on the kind of work he or she would like to do abroad, this may be the best option. It can be a wonderful experience to design your own trip and project, especially if you have a unique schedule or already know the area you are traveling to. Just remember that the longer you stay in a community, the greater the difference you can make. Most of the organizations we have listed in this book are based in the US or Europe and make international connections for their volunteers. However, there are thousands of NGOs, both small and large, all over the world, and we could not possibly include all of them here.

You can begin by researching grassroots organizations and contacting them to find out more about their needs and the types of skills they can use. When designing your own experience, it is important to think carefully about the specific skills you can bring to an organization and to be upfront about what you can offer to the organizations you contact. A volunteer who went to work with a community organization in Mexico learned that his most useful skill was puppet making. He didn't know before he arrived that street theater is a popular form of political communication. When a local clinic learned that he was an artist and an actor, they suggested that he help them communicate health care information through puppet shows.

In the Resources section of this book, we have included several publications and websites that list NGOs and other volunteer opportunities. The Internet is an invaluable resource for finding organizations. After spending an hour or two searching, you will probably have several organizations to contact, and you can begin to narrow your search depending on the needs and values of each organization.

While researching and making connections from home is essential, it may be that you need to wait until you are in-country to figure out the details of your volunteer experience. Many small NGOs do not have Internet access, and you can only learn about them once you are there. The most important thing for you to do when you are working independently is to talk to people. The more people you meet and learn from, the more connections you will make and the more doors will open.

Keep in mind that it is a mistake to assume that all grassroots organizations need or want volunteers. Some groups are suspicious of the idea of unpaid labor in any context and prefer to retain only a tiny but paid staff. Some emphasize the values of mutual aid and local empowerment to the point of not wanting volunteers from outside the community served. Do not presume that, with a little coaxing or bargaining, you can overcome the resistance of someone who says no to your offer to volunteer. When you contact organizations, clearly state your goals, expectations, skills, and the length of time you are available. The organization can then decide if you can be of service in its work.

What Are Your Motivations?

Before committing to an organization, it is important to clarify your motives and your constraints. You may be drawn to voluntary service by a desire to help people striving for social, political, or economic change; you may be interested in learning about another culture and society; you may seek adventure; you may be eager to gain experience that will help you find a job. Your motivation may consist of all these reasons and more, to varying degrees. Thoroughly understanding why you want to volunteer can help you find a good organization, keep you focused and confident during your service, and ensure that you get the most from the experience.

Humanitarian motivations lead many prospective volunteers to communities plagued by extreme poverty and injustice. A volunteer may wish to feed the hungry, heal the sick, or house the homeless, but these social and political problems are often incredibly complex. Learning the dynamics of a community is the greatest challenge to a volunteer, making the volunteer's most appropriate role that of a student. An ill-advised motivation for volunteering can sometimes accompany the humanitarian impulse. This motivation might be called crusaderism—wanting to travel to far-flung pockets of deprivation and change everything in the space of three months. To expect too much from your volunteer experience is to set yourself up for disappointment. We might do well to heed the observation of Dorothy Day, cofounder of the Catholic Worker Movement in the 1930s, who assessed the slow pace of social change: "What we do is so little that we may seem to be constantly failing. . . . And why must we see the results of our giving? Our work is to sow—another generation will be reaping the harvest."

Concerned American citizens who want to help impoverished people don't need to travel around the globe to fulfill their goals. The challenges of community development here at home are immense. For this reason, one section of this book is dedicated to US organizations. Voluntary service in low-income communities in the US can also be a valuable educational experience or preparation for future work.

Another motivation for voluntary service is the desire to learn more about other societies. Living in another country can build your appreciation of the richness of other cultures and enable you to gain a comparative perspective on life in the United States. Apart from formal long-term volunteering, work brigades, study tours, and international education programs offer short-term exposure and, often, a component of historical and theoretical insight into problems faced by the communities you visit. Many such programs are specifically designed for students. In this book, a number of tour, education, and shorter-term programs are also listed in the Alternative Travel and Study Overseas section.

If your concern is to improve your qualifications for a career in development, an unconventional work experience may enhance your candidacy. The best programs place volunteers with local NGOs that have requested a volunteer for a specific purpose. In these circumstances, volunteers have a better chance of making a meaningful contribution. These placements often require some skills—computer, teaching, agriculture, appropriate technology, health care, or fundraising. If you do not already have experience in these areas, it would be wise to develop specific technical skills that may be of use to an organization, as well as language competency.

Simple escapism—the desire to get away from home to evade personal problems or because you can't decide on a career—is an understandable impulse, but it's not the best motivation for volunteering. If you are troubled, preoccupied, or at loose ends, your effectiveness overseas will be diminished.

Evaluating an Organization

The listings in this book describe dozens of organizations that we think offer strong alternatives for overseas and domestic volunteer experiences. But the listings are just a start. In addition to this book, many resources are available for finding organizations on your own, such as the Internet, career counseling centers, your friends, and other books. A few ideas are listed in the Resources section at the back of this book. Take the time to explore the myriad of opportunities available, both in this book and beyond, to find the organization or project best suited to your needs, motivations, and skills. No matter which voluntary service organization you are considering, it is important to ask questions that allow you to evaluate its motives, methods, and effectiveness. You want to be sure that the organization you devote your time and energy to is in line with your goals and values before you commit to working with them. To help you in this process, here are some questions based on those we used to evaluate the organizations included in this book. You may think of others that will help you match an organization's values to your own.

- What is the political or religious affiliation of the organization? Is its purpose to convert or influence poor people to adopt new cultural, economic, or social values?

- What is the organization's mission statement? How does it actually work to accomplish its goals?

- Will you be taking a job that could be done by a local person? If you are offering a new skill to an area, does the program involve transferring that skill to local people? Are the organization's goals to make the program self-sustainable?

- Who funds the organization? Do the funding sources have political or religious affiliations that may influence the organization's programs?

- How does the organization choose its programs? Have local people requested help from volunteers? Or do staff, funders, or the organization's board determine its programs?

- Is the organization working with local or national governments?

- If the organization says it works with local groups or NGOs, find out what types of groups they mean and what type of partnership they have. For example, the organization might work with a local school on an environmental education project or with a women's group working for economic self-sufficiency.

- What sort of training and support can you expect as a volunteer?

To answer questions like these, look beyond the program's brochures. If possible, get a list of previous volunteers and ask them about their experiences. Did they get good training and support? Was the experience what they expected based on the organization's claims, and, if not, why not? You may also want to write to people in the field, finding out who is critical of the program and why. The section called Further Reading lists several books that take a critical look at development organizations overseas.

Whether you decide on an organized volunteer program, a tour, or to go on your own, it is essential to do your homework beforehand. Read as much as possible about the country (especially its history and politics), learn about groups working in the area, write in advance to groups that interest you, and talk to people at home who know about the area you are considering.

Fundraising

One of the biggest challenges that comes with choosing an alternative to the Peace Corps is finding a way to finance your trip. While some agencies offer a stipend, insurance, or travel expenses, many smaller programs are not able to offer these benefits. Government or church organizations can often afford to be more generous, and this is a major reason people choose to work through those organizations. Making your desire to work at the grassroots level a reality will require a creative approach to fundraising. Particularly if you choose to work with a small, local organization, it is highly unlikely that they will be able to help you with your expenses. Truthfully, they cannot afford to put their resources anywhere but directly into the community in which they are working.

The first thing you should do is come up with a tentative, itemized budget for your trip. Research the potential costs of each of your expenses before you begin fundraising. Not only does this give you a goal to reach in your fundraising efforts, it shows those you are asking that you have given thought to your budget and are asking for money you will actually need.

Below is a list of many of the items you should include:

- Transportation to and from the site (airline tickets are often the biggest expense for a trip to a nation where housing and food costs are minimal compared to the US)

- Program fee (consult the program you are interested in to find out what fee, if any, they require)

- Housing costs

- Food costs

- Transportation during your stay (buses, trains, etc.)

- Communication costs (stamps, phone cards, Internet fees)

- Spending money

- Medical insurance

- Visa fee

- Medicine

- Departure tax (from the airport abroad)

- Travel gear (this includes anything you may need to buy, such as mosquito nets, water filters, camping equipment, etc.)

- Passport application fee

- Other (e.g., student loan repayments or other obligations)

Airfare will be your primary expense; living in a developing nation, especially in rural areas, is by and large extremely affordable in comparison to living expenses in the US. If you can arrange an internship or a work exchange (like teaching English) for room and board, your living expenses can be kept to a minimum. Ask the organization you'll be working with for suggestions about this, though it will probably be easier to arrange a work exchange once you are in-country. The best way to find out how much money you should expect to need for some of these items, such as transportation and spending money, is to ask people who have worked or lived in the area you are traveling to. Ask the organization you are going to work with, and volunteers who have worked with the organization in the past, about costs.

Once you have figured out an estimated budget, don't let the numbers daunt you! You can go about finding the funds to support your trip in several ways, and if you make a fundraising plan and stick to it, you are very likely to raise the funds you need. Your plan should include efforts to raise funds from several sources (some of which are described below). Approaching several sources in a thoughtful manner will bring success more quickly than putting all your eggs in one basket and hoping for the best. Successful fundraising requires equal parts research, creativity, perseverance, and willingness to ask for help.

Scholarships and Fellowships

These are often available through universities, and if you are enrolled in school, you should find out what resources are available for students wishing to travel to research or volunteer abroad. Universities also offer stipends toward room and board expenses for internships or volunteer programs in the US. Public libraries, career service centers, and specialized libraries like the Foundation Center—which has branches throughout the country—are sources for information on grants and loans for anyone. You may also be able to find funding through your local government, private associations, or church groups. For example, the Rotary Club offers scholarships for foreign travel, and many churches support their parishioners in return for educational services upon return from an overseas trip.

Loans and Gifts

Friends and relatives are another possible source of funds. You may be able to arrange a personal loan, or ask your extended circle for small contributions using a well-written fundraising letter that describes your project and what you'll use the money for.

Events and Exchanges

Consider organizing a fundraising pancake breakfast, bake sale, or white elephant sale. Friends, family, club or church members, or local businesses may be willing to help you by donating time, space, food, services, or items for sale. One woman who traveled throughout Central America for a year started her own newsletter and asked friends and family to subscribe to help subsidize her living expenses. If you receive funding from individuals or organizations, your funders may appreciate a slide show or talk about your experiences upon your return—or, if you're inclined, start a weblog that will help them share your experiences as they happen.

Your Own Resources

One source of funds (maybe the main source) will be your own bank account. Part of your fundraising plan will probably include working for a while to save money for a trip or using savings you already have. You may also consider selling some possessions to help finance your travels.

Bringing the Lessons to Life

Working with poor communities, whether at home or abroad, to confront the causes of hunger and poverty can have a long-lasting impact on your life. It can deepen your understanding of the tremendous power the US has over the lives of people around the world: to make and break governments; to affect the world economy through trade, investment, and foreign aid policies; and to influence economic priorities through USAID, the World Bank, the International Monetary Fund, and the World Trade Organization, among other entities.

The work will be educational, but that is only the beginning. Experience with a disenfranchised community means taking the responsibility of bringing your experiences home. The lessons you learn may have direct applications: working to end hunger and poverty in the US, pressuring the US government to end its involvement with repressive regimes, limiting arms sales to developing nations, and holding US corporations accountable for their actions, whether overseas or at home.

An experience in a developing nation can be translated into work at home in many ways. A Peace Corps volunteer who served with Guatemalan Indians returned to the US and worked with Native Americans in Arizona. A health-care volunteer with an international organization in Ghana found work at a free clinic in California. An agricultural extension worker who volunteered in Mozambique became active in the movement to stop US support of South Africa's apartheid regime. These examples and others show that experience in a marginalized community is often the catalyst for taking action in your own country to create more democratic organizations and politics at the local, national, and international levels, and to help ensure the survival of grassroots efforts all over the world.

How to Use This Book

In compiling the following lists of organizations, we looked for groups that address the political and economic causes of poverty. In our view, these programs place volunteers in positions that complement the work of local people, grassroots organizations, and nongovernmental organizations (NGOs) by focusing on capacity building and providing services that are sustainable.

We made a few significant discriminations when deciding which organizations to include in the book. Organizations that rely on US government funding are not included because government money can never be completely free from Washington's agendas. A command of the English language has without question become a desirable attainment in many developing nations, but we list none of the organizations that deal strictly in sending English teachers overseas. We include only a few of the organizations devoted to sending teachers abroad, on the grounds that most of those programs serve primarily the host countries' middle or professional classes. We have tried to steer clear of any organizations that are evangelical, but we do list some volunteer programs with religious affiliations that hold as their primary purpose the support of local efforts at community development. Some do require a commitment to a certain faith, but most ask only that the volunteer share a concern for social justice. As with any volunteer placement, it is important to understand the values behind an agency's volunteer program clearly. We have done the initial screening, but you should investigate an organization thoroughly before you choose to work with them.

The listings are by no means comprehensive. Many organizations are so small and take so few volunteers that they prefer not to be listed, which is not to say that they would not like to be approached by informed and enterprising potential volunteers. Hundreds of other possibilities are not mentioned because they are so locally based that it makes more sense to find and contact them once you are abroad. We were only able to include a fraction of the organizations doing good work around the globe, so this book should be a launching point in your search for volunteer opportunities and commitment to social justice. Every community, school, church, and labor union has the potential for developing international programs that send delegates abroad, initiate ongoing partnership programs, and offer direct assistance to communities in developing nations or underserved communities in the US. These opportunities are often the most exciting, but must be created by the volunteer. (See the Designing Your Own Experience section in chapter 2 for more information.)

The organizations in this book are divided into four sections. The first two sections, International Voluntary Service Organizations and US Voluntary Service Organizations, are self-explanatory. In the Alternative Travel and Study Overseas section, you'll find organizations that sponsor short-term work projects, educational travel to frequently inaccessible areas of the world, and opportunities to study abroad. The last section, Resources, includes other organizations and guides, which do not sponsor regular volunteer programs but may distribute information or serve as a resource in your search.

We've added a few tools to this edition of *Alternatives to the Peace Corps* to aid you in using the book and searching for the best volunteer opportunity for you. There are two indexes at the back of the book, one alphabetical and one geographical. If you are looking for a volunteer program in a specific region of the world, refer to the geographical index. You will find icons beside the entries for many organizations included in this book to help you narrow your search quickly. The icons are meant to be a resource for you, but not a definitive word on any of these organizations. You should contact organizations directly with specific questions. A key for the icons appears on the next page.

Key to Icons

R All of these organizations have a religious affiliation. Buddhism, Catholicism, and Judaism are just a few of the faith groups represented in this book. Some organizations are affiliated with a specific religious tradition, while others identify as interfaith. Most of these organizations do not require their volunteers be of a certain faith, and the emphasis on religion varies greatly among these groups.

These organizations request proficiency in a foreign language for participation in some or all of their programs. While some of these organizations require fluency in a foreign language, some say knowledge of a foreign language is helpful but not necessary.

These organizations offer some short-term volunteer opportunities of one month or less. (This icon does not appear in the Alternative Travel and Study Overseas section because most of the organizations listed in that section offer *only* short-term opportunities.)

These organizations all offer some kind of financial assistance to their volunteers. This ranges from groups that offer complete coverage of all expenses, including airfare, to organizations that provide modest monthly stipends abroad, to groups that offer a very limited number of scholarships.

PART II

Organizations and Resources

Key to Icons

See page 29 for full description.

R   Religious affiliation.

◯   Foreign language proficiency requested.

◔   Short-term volunteer opportunities available.

📖   Financial assistance available.

International Voluntary
Service Organizations

The following organizations offer opportunities to work abroad on a wide variety of issues and projects. These voluntary service organizations are selected for their common approach to combating injustices, emphasizing support of grassroots efforts around the globe. They are building international cooperation through the empowerment and leadership of local people.

Adventures in Health, Education, and Agricultural Development, Inc.
PO Box 2049, Rockville, MD 20847-2049
Tel: (301) 530-3697
Fax: (301) 530-3532
E-mail: info@aheadinc.org
Website: www.aheadinc.org

Adventures in Health, Education, and Agricultural Development (AHEAD) combats malnutrition, disease, and poverty through people-to-people exchanges and support of grassroots initiatives. Since 1985, AHEAD has provided opportunities for professionals and graduate and undergraduate students to work as volunteers side-by-side with their African counterparts in community projects in rural Tanzania and the Gambia. AHEAD's programs emphasize child survival and safe motherhood, focusing on teen pregnancy prevention, HIV/AIDS and STD prevention, immunizations, nutrition, family planning, women's health, and youth leadership development.

The summer volunteer program for undergraduates runs six to eight weeks and costs $4,000, airfare included. Length and cost of programs for graduates and professionals vary; contact AHEAD for details. Volunteers are encouraged to fundraise for their trips. All contributions to AHEAD, Inc., are tax-deductible.

Agencia Latinoamericana de Información

12 de octubre N18-24 y Patria, Of 503, Quito, Ecuador
(Mailing address: Casilla 17-12-877, Quito, Ecuador)
Tel: 011 (593 2) 250-5074 or 011 (593 2) 222-1570
Fax: 011 (593 2) 250-5073
E-mail: info@alainet.org
Website: www.alainet.org
Contact: Sally Burch, executive director

The Agencia Latinoamericana de Información (ALAI) is a communications organization committed to human rights, gender equality, and people's participation in the development of Latin America. ALAI works for the democratization of communication. To that end, it has developed a model of alternative communication that aims toward the formation of a new fabric of communication that is democratic, widespread, decentralized, and multicultural.

ALAI accepts a few volunteers in its Quito office each year. Volunteers may assist with translation or documentation work for ALAI's publications and website, or help design ALAI's website and databases. Volunteers are expected to cover their own expenses.

American Friends Service Committee

1501 Cherry Street, Philadelphia, PA 19102-1479
Tel: (215) 241-7295
Fax: (215) 241-7247
E-mail: mexsummer@afsc.org
Website: www.afsc.org

American Friends Service Committee (AFSC) sponsors summer programs in Mexico for people ages eighteen to twenty-six. AFSC's goals are to promote understanding across divisions of history, economics, and culture; to assist communities as they develop resources; and to provide young adults from different backgrounds with an opportunity to grow personally and to develop career-related skills. The community service program in Mexico runs from early July to the end of August. Participants live in rural villages. They work under the direction of Mexican organizations and respond to the needs of the particular community in which they live. Applicants should have skills in construction, gardening, arts, crafts, child care, or other practical areas. Proficiency in Spanish is necessary. Prior experience in community service and organizing is very helpful. Participants pay a $1,250 fee for seven weeks and cover their own travel expenses. A limited number of scholarships are available, as are several paid facilitator positions. AFSC is a Quaker organization.

Amigos de las Americas

5618 Star Lane, Houston, TX 77057
Tel: (800) 231-7796
Fax: (713) 782-9267
E-mail: info@amigoslink.org
Website: www.amigoslink.org

Amigos de las Americas is an international, volunteer-driven, nonprofit organization that builds partnerships to empower young leaders, advance community development, and strengthen multicultural understanding in the Americas. Amigos accepts volunteers sixteen years or older to work in teams in Latin America during the summer months. Programs run for four to eight weeks. Volunteers provide health, education, and community development services to communities in eight Latin American countries (Mexico, Costa Rica, the Dominican Republic, Nicaragua, Paraguay, Brazil, Honduras, and Bolivia). In addition to bringing technical knowledge and supplies to the project, volunteers assume leadership roles as health educators. Amigos chapters across the US conduct training prior to departure and raise funds for the majority of volunteers. Individuals who do not live in cities with chapters can apply as correspondent volunteers through the headquarters in Houston. The cost is approximately $3,400 to $3,800, but may vary depending on the area of placement. Fundraising is strongly encouraged, and financial assistance based on need is available. The fee covers all expenses, including international airfare from Houston or Miami, housing with a family, food, transportation, and short-term medical insurance. At least two years of high school Spanish or the equivalent is required. Current project information can be found on the website.

Amizade, Ltd.
920 William Pitt Union, Pittsburgh, PA 15260
Tel: (888) 973-4443 or (412) 648-1488
Fax: (412) 648-1492
E-mail: volunteer@amizade.org
Website: www.amizade.org

Amizade encourages intercultural exploration and understanding through community-driven service-learning courses and volunteer programs.

In communities on five continents, over 1,000 Amizade volunteers have cooperated with community members to complete sustainable, community-identified projects that address needs in education, the environment, and health and well-being. Within the context of a unique cross-cultural experience that offers educational and recreational opportunities, Amizade volunteers have constructed an orphanage that houses forty children in Bolivia, built a vocational training center for street children in the Brazilian Amazon, and completed historical restoration and environmental preservation in the Greater Yellowstone Area. Volunteers do not need any special skills, just a willingness to help. Current opportunities exist in Australia, Bolivia, Brazil, Nepal, the US, and in several other communities around the world.

Amizade offers prescheduled programs for individuals and customized programs for groups. Additionally, through a partnership with the University of Pittsburgh, the Amizade Global Service-Learning Center facilitates courses that combine intercultural service and academic coursework for college credit. Volunteer program fees range from $475 to $1,895. The program fee includes room and board; transportation during the program; recreational, cultural, and educational activities; Amizade staff and administration fees; and a donation to the community.

Bikes Not Bombs
(See listing under US Voluntary Service Organizations)

Brethren Volunteer Service   R ✒ ◯
1451 Dundee Avenue, Elgin, IL 60120
Tel: (847) 742-5100 or (800) 323-8039
Fax: (847) 742-6103
E-mail: bvs_gb@brethren.org
Website: www.brethrenvolunteerservice.org

Brethren Volunteer Service (BVS) is a program grounded in the Christian faith that brings a spiritual dimension to advocating justice, working for peace, serving basic human needs, and maintaining the integrity of creation. BVS places volunteers in Latin America, Europe, Asia, and Africa. BVS also has one-year programs in the US. Positions abroad last two years and begin with a three-week orientation in the US. Volunteers are involved in a variety of community services: education, health care, office/secretarial work, and construction work. Volunteers can also participate in ministry to children, youth, senior citizens, homeless, victims of domestic violence, prisoners, refugees, and persons with AIDS. Some positions require knowledge of a foreign language prior to orientation. Other requirements and special skills vary with assignments. Volunteers need not be Brethren or Christian but should be willing to examine the Christian faith. A college degree or equivalent life experience is required for overseas assignments. Travel expenses, room and board, medical coverage, and a monthly stipend of about $60 are provided.

Building Responsible International Dialogue through Grassroots Exchanges

1203 Preservation Park, Suite 300, Oakland CA 94612
Tel: (510) 271-8286
Fax: (510) 451-2996
E-mail: information@grassrootsbridges.org
Website: www.grassrootsbridges.org

Building Responsible International Dialogue through Grassroots Exchanges (BRIDGES) supports young community organizers from low-income and ethnically diverse backgrounds to increase their capacity for direct grassroots organizing, with a vision centered on global justice. Through extensive training and mentorship, plus international travel and internship placements, BRIDGES builds responsible international dialogues for grassroots communities in the US and the global South to exchange ideas on sustainable solutions to common issues. The program is centered on principles of participatory education, cultural work, and understanding through personal experience. Applicants must be at least eighteen years of age, US citizens or residents with demonstrated financial need, have worked for positive change in their communities, have had limited opportunity to travel abroad, and have no previous international volunteer experience.

BRIDGES also hosts delegations from human rights and popular education NGOs from Guatemala for young grassroots organizers from the global South to share in their own voice their experiences of resistance and liberation. BRIDGES is available to provide training for other organizations and school groups conducting their own international exchanges.

Center for Political and Economic Research for Community Action

(Centro de Investigaciones Económicas y Políticas de Acción Comunitaria, A.C.)

Calle de la Primavera, No. 6, Barrio de la Merced C.P. 29240,
San Cristóbal de las Casas, Chiapas, Mexico
Tel/Fax: 011 (52) 967-674-5168
E-mail: ciepac@laneta.apc.org
Website: www.ciepac.org
Contact: Gabriela Soriana, general coordinator

The Center for Political and Economic Research for Community Action (CIEPAC) is an alternative to mainstream sources of information in Mexico, empowering citizens and citizen organizations to use information to create their own analysis, spaces for participation, and alternatives. Projects include weekly analysis bulletins, grassroots analysis forums with indigenous communities, education of the "first world" and elaboration of popular education materials, all to strengthen local, national, and international movements for justice.

CIEPAC usually accepts volunteers to work in their office every six months. Volunteers work on translations of analysis and popular education materials from Spanish to English or other languages, and also may help with research or writing about the effects of globalization on the communities in Chiapas, depending on their experience and expertise. Volunteers should be proficient in Spanish and are expected to pay all costs.

Child Family Health International

953 Mission Street, Suite 220, San Francisco, CA 94103
Tel: (415) 957-9000
Fax: (501) 432 – 6852
E-mail: info@cfhi.org
Website: www.cfhi.org

Child Family Health International (CFHI) is a nonprofit organization providing health services to underserved communities worldwide by supporting local projects with essential medical supplies, volunteers, and funding. CFHI sends US medical, premedical, nursing and other public health students to Ecuador, Mexico, South Africa, and India for training and service learning. Duties include hospital or clinical rotations and community education and outreach.

Participants should view their experience as an opportunity to develop cross-cultural and community health awareness, rather than to provide humanitarian aid. Programs vary in length from three to twelve weeks. Spanish language proficiency is useful for many of the placements, though language courses often are included in the program. Scholarships are available on a limited basis. Fees vary by program. Refer to the website for more detail.

Christian Peacemaker Teams   R 🐾 ☉

PO Box 6508, Chicago, IL 60680-6508
Tel: (773) 277-0253
Fax: (773) 277-0291
E-mail: cpt@igc.org
Website: www.prairienet.org/cpt

Christian Peacemaker Teams (CPT) places teams of international volunteers in conflict settings as a violence-reduction presence. CPT is cross-denominational, with strong roots grounded in the Quakers, Mennonites, and Church of the Brethren. CPT organizes long-term volunteers—the Christian Peacemaker Corps—to perform protective witness and accompaniment work in the West Bank, Chiapas, Vieques, Colombia, and Native American communities in the US and Canada. Teams of two to twelve persons join the efforts of local peacemakers facing imminent violence. They accompany threatened individuals, report on human rights abuses, plan and execute nonviolent public responses to injustice, and train others in nonviolent direct action.

CPT emphasizes the Christian nature of its commitment to peace. All Christian Peacemaker Corps volunteers must attend training in nonviolent direct action, either at CPT headquarters in Chicago or at regional sessions offered if demand is sufficient. Candidates pay their own way to training; if accepted, full-time corps members receive a small monthly stipend based on their living expenses and are expected to seek contributions to CPT in support of their work. CPT also maintains a reserve corps of trained volunteers on-call for short periods of time. Corps volunteers and reservists must be twenty-one or older.

(See listing under Alternative Travel and Study Overseas)

Christians for Peace in El Salvador   R

122 DeWitt Drive, Boston, MA 02120
Tel: (617) 445-5115
Fax: (617) 249-0769
E-mail: info@crispaz.org
Website: www.crispaz.org

Founded in 1984, Christians for Peace in El Salvador, or CRISPAZ, is a faith-based organization dedicated to working with poor and marginalized communities in El Salvador. In building bridges of solidarity between communities in El Salvador and those in their home countries, CRISPAZ volunteers strive together for peace, justice, and human liberation. The long-term volunteer program is designed for individuals who wish to spend a minimum of one year living and working in a marginalized urban or rural community in El Salvador. Long-term volunteers give of their time, skills, and interests as they work alongside Salvadorans in areas such as literacy, health care, pastoral work, community organization, education, agriculture, appropriate technology, and youth work. The summer immersion program is designed to provide an intensive learning and service experience in a poor community in El Salvador. Interns live with Salvadorans and accompany them in their daily lives and work. Each intern will have the opportunity to contribute his or her skills to the communities. CRISPAZ provides volunteers with orientation, project placement, and support throughout the term of service.

(See listing under Alternative Travel and Study Overseas)

Concern America

2015 North Broadway, Santa Ana, CA 92706
Mailing address: PO Box 1790, Santa Ana, CA 92702
Tel: (714) 953-8575 or (800) 266-2376
Fax: (714) 953-1242
E-mail: concamerinc@earthlink.net
Website: www.concernamerica.org

Concern America is an international development and refugee aid organization whose main objective is to provide training, technical assistance, and material support to community-based programs in developing countries and refugee camps. Concern America volunteers serve for at least two years and are professionals such as physicians, nurses, nutritionists, community organizers, and specialists in agriculture, appropriate technology, public health, and sanitation. The focus of the work is on training local people to carry on programs that include health-care training, developing nutrition and sanitation projects, organizing community development and income-generating projects, and conducting literacy campaigns. Concern America volunteers currently serve in El Salvador, Honduras, Guatemala, Mexico, and Mozambique. Volunteers must be at least twenty-one and fluent in Spanish. Concern America provides transportation, room and board, health insurance, and a small stipend. In addition, a repatriation allowance of $50 per month of service is provided to the volunteer upon completion of contract.

Cross-Cultural Solutions

47 Potter Avenue, New Rochelle, NY 10801
Tel: (800) 380-4777 or (914) 632-0022
Fax: (914) 632-8494
E-mail: info@crossculturalsolutions.org
Website: www.crossculturalsolutions.org

Cross-Cultural Solutions' international volunteer programs let you experience a country from a whole new perspective. Programs are available in Brazil, China, Costa Rica, Ghana, India, Peru, Russia, Thailand, and Tanzania; Cross-Cultural Solutions is continuing to open new programs in areas around the world. They believe that people know and understand what is appropriate for their own communities. By participating in a Cross-Cultural Solutions program, volunteers have the opportunity to work side-by-side with local people on locally designed and driven projects. This type of interaction leads to the sharing of perspectives and the fostering of cultural understanding, which are both essential parts of Cross-Cultural Solutions' mission.

Cross-Cultural Solutions volunteers are placed individually with locally based partner programs. They work on sustainable community development projects with infants and children, teenagers, adults, the elderly, and people with special needs like HIV/AIDS patients or the mentally or physically disabled. Cross-Cultural Solutions provides programming meant to give the volunteer a holistic view of the complexities that create the local culture, including an in-depth orientation, insight into cultural norms, language assistance, guest speakers who are experts in their fields, and special events. Volunteers have free time most evenings and every weekend to reflect on their experience and become more familiar with the local people and culture.

Cross-Cultural Solutions has a home-base structure in each country, including local staff from the community, lodging, meals, and transportation. Cross-Cultural Solutions' international volunteer programs range from two to twelve weeks (longer programs can be arranged). The program fee starts at $1,985 and is tax-deductible in the US.

Doctors for Global Health

PO Box 1761, Decatur, GA 30031
Tel/Fax: (404) 377-3566
E-mail: volunteer@dghonline.org
Website: www.dghonline.org

Doctors for Global Health (DGH) is a private, not-for-profit organization promoting health and human rights with those who have no voice. Founded in 1995, DGH strives to promote health, education, social justice, and human rights by funding and carrying out projects in cooperation with local nonprofit and nongovernmental partner organizations in interested communities. With an emphasis on community-oriented primary care, liberation medicine, and volunteerism, DGH accompanies communities in El Salvador, Nicaragua, Mexico, Peru, Uganda, and the United States. Various volunteer opportunities are available, depending on the volunteer's skills and the needs and desires of the local community. Most volunteer activities involve health care, education, and public health activities. DGH prefers long-term volunteers but does occasionally accept volunteers for minimum stays of one to two months. Volunteers should expect to pay for their own travel expenses, food, and lodging.

Doctors Without Borders USA, Inc.   ♡

Médecins Sans Frontières USA, Inc.
In New York:
333 7th Avenue, 2nd Floor, New York, NY 10001-5004
Tel: (212) 679-6800 or (888) 392-0392
Fax: (212) 679-7016
E-mail: doctors@newyork.msf.org
Website: www.doctorswithoutborders.org
In Los Angeles:
2525 Main Street, Suite 110, Santa Maria, CA 90405
Tel: (310) 399-0049
Fax: (310) 399-8177
E-mail: msf-losangeles@msf.org

Doctors Without Borders (known internationally as Médecins Sans Frontières, or MSF) is the world's largest independent emergency medical relief organization. Each year over 2,000 doctors, nurses, other medical professionals, and logistical experts from forty-five nations volunteer to work in more than eighty countries around the world. They assist victims of war, civil strife, epidemics, and natural disasters, without discrimination of race, religion, creed, or political affiliation.

Solid professional experience is essential in the field. All medical professionals must have a valid license to practice and must have had two years of post-graduate professional work experience. The minimum volunteer commitment is six months; a year's commitment is more typical. A good working knowledge of a foreign language is highly valued. Familiarity with tropical medicine is an asset. For more information or an application form, please call or visit the website.

Fellowship of Reconciliation   R
Task Force on Latin America and the Caribbean

2017 Mission Street, #305, San Francisco, CA 94110
Tel: (415) 495-6334
Fax: (415) 495-5628
E-mail: forcolombia@igc.org
Website: www.forusa.org/programs/Colombia

The Fellowship of Reconciliation (FOR) is accepting applications for volunteers to accompany the Peace Community of San José de Apartadó, in Colombia's northern region of Urabá. San José de Apartadó is one of some fifty communities in Colombia that has taken an extraordinary and nonviolent stand against war, by refusing to support any armed actor involved in Colombia's decades-long conflict. The community has suffered terribly from political violence, and its agricultural center, La Unión, has been victim to repeated paramilitary attacks. The Peace Community has requested FOR volunteers to accompany them in their nonviolent resistance. To ensure the continuity of this presence, FOR seeks committed and skilled volunteers ready to share the lives of these people striving for a life in peace and dignity. FOR is an interfaith organization.

Focus on the Global South

(See listing under Resources)

Foundation for Sustainable Development
59 Driftwood Court, San Rafael, CA 94901
Tel/Fax: (415) 482-9366
E-mail: info@fsdinternational.org
Website: www.fsdinternational.org

The Foundation for Sustainable Development (FSD) is a private nonprofit organization dedicated to supporting sustainable development initiatives in Latin America and Africa. Programs include an internship with a nonprofit development organization, family homestay, orientation and debriefing, and in some cases language training and group trips. Programs stress complete immersion and place only one intern in each organization and family. While internship programs are available throughout the year, for two months to one year, the summer programs have set dates and last between nine and ten weeks. Internships are available in a variety of areas and include education, community development, human rights, environment/conservation, microfinance, women's issues, health, nutrition, youth development, and many more. Programs are located in Bolivia, Ecuador, Nicaragua, Peru, Tanzania, and Uganda. For more information about the application process and for internship descriptions, please see the website. Program costs vary. Credit and scholarships may be available.

Fourth World Movement

7600 Willow Hill Drive, Landover, MD 20785-4658
Tel: (301) 336-9489
Fax: (301) 336-0092
E-mail: fourthworld@erols.com
Website: www.atd-fourthworld.org

Fourth World Movement's work is based on three priorities: learning from the most disadvantaged families, understanding how they become trapped in persistent poverty, and planning and developing projects with them. Volunteers must first participate in a two- to three-month internship living and working with full-time volunteers at the New York, New Orleans, and Washington, DC, area centers. Interns learn about Fourth World Movement and its approach to persistent poverty through their work, and through videos, readings and discussion. At the end of the internship, interns discuss with their supervisor what their two-year assignment will be. Placement is made according to both the interns' interests and Fourth World's needs. There are currently teams in twenty-six countries and six continents. Participants contribute toward food costs during the internship and receive a small stipend during their assignment.

(See listing under Alternative Travel and Study Overseas)

Frontier Internship in Mission **R**

International Coordinating Office
Ecumenical Center
150 Route de Ferney, 1211 Geneva 2, Switzerland
Tel: 41 (22) 798-8987
Fax: 41 (22) 788-1434
E-mail: jm@tfim.org
Website: www.tfim.org

Frontier Internship in Mission (FIM) is an international ecumenical internship program that provides people between twenty and thirty-five years of age with the opportunity to work abroad on social issues for two years. The program emphasizes new forms of ecumenical mission in the context of justice, peace, and the ecosphere. FIM supports community building, especially among poor people's organizations in Asia, Africa, and Latin America. Individuals applying to FIM should be members of a community engaged in justice concerns. Communities interested in receiving an intern propose a project to

FIM; communities wanting to send an intern to another region may also apply. The FIM coordinating office funds travel expenses, provides a subsistence living allowance, and coordinates a one-year reentry project with the intern's sending group after the two-year period overseas.

Frontiers Foundation/Operation Beaver

419 Coxwell Avenue, Toronto, Ontario M4L-3B9 Canada
Tel: (416) 690-3930
Fax: (416) 690-3934
E-mail: frontiersfoundation@on.aibn.com
Website: www.frontiersfoundation.org

Frontiers Foundation is a community development service organization that works in partnership with communities in low-income rural areas across northern Canada. These locally initiated projects build and improve housing, conduct training programs, and organize educational and recreational activities in developing regions. Volunteers must be eighteen or older and available for a minimum of twelve weeks. Skills in carpentry, electrical work, and plumbing are preferred for construction projects. Previous social service and experience with children are preferred for recreation and education projects. Accommodations, food, and travel inside Canada are provided.

Global Routes

1 Short Street, Northampton, MA 01060
Tel: (413) 585-8895
Fax: (413) 585-8810
E-mail: mail@globalroutes.org
Website: www.globalroutes.org

Global Routes is a nonprofit, nongovernmental organization that designs teaching internships and community service programs in rural communities throughout the world for North American high school and college age students. Participants live and work with their host families on projects selected by the community. These have included constructing schools, clinics, and community centers, as well as teaching. High school programs currently exist in Belize, Costa Rica, the Dominican Republic, Ecuador, Guadeloupe, Ghana, Kenya, St. Lucia, Thailand, and the United States. These programs are four to six weeks long in the summer. College programs are offered in Costa Rica, Ecuador, Ghana, Kenya, St. Lucia, and Thailand. These programs are three months long (fall, winter, and summer). Participants pay all program expenses.

Global Volunteer Network

PO Box 2231, Wellington, New Zealand
Tel: 011 (64 4) 569-9080
Fax: 011 (64 4) 569-9081
E-mail: info@volunteer.org.nz
Website: www.volunteer.org.nz
Contact: Colin Salisbury, executive director

Global Volunteer Network supports local community organizations in developing countries through the placement of international volunteers. Currently opportunities are available in China, Ecuador, Ghana, Nepal, New Zealand, Romania, Russia, and Thailand. Volunteers can be involved in areas such as teaching English, environmental work, animal welfare, and health education. Volunteers can participate in cultural homestays as well. Program placement ranges from two weeks to twelve months and is available to those over the age of seventeen. No previous experience is necessary. The application fee is $250, followed by monthly program fees that range from $250 to $600. Contact the executive director for more information.

Kim Rollinson, Volunteer, Global Volunteer Network

I volunteered in Ghana, West Africa, and was there for approximately five weeks in spring 2002 then again for five weeks in summer 2002 (I went back because I loved it so much). I was staying in a small fishing village on the coast and was teaching mainly English and sciences in a junior/secondary school there. I loved the time I spent there and made some brilliant friends for life. It was great to just absorb the different lifestyle and actually live the life with the locals rather than being a tourist looking in from the outside.

Global Volunteers

375 East Little Canada Road, St. Paul, MN 55117-1627
Tel: (800) 487-1074 or (651) 407-6100
Fax: (651) 482-0915
E-mail: email@globalvolunteers.org
Website: www.globalvolunteers.org

Global Volunteers forms teams of volunteers who live in host communities and work with local people on development projects selected by local leadership. The projects may involve construction and renovation of schools and clinics, health care, tutoring, business planning, or assisting in other local activities. Opportunities are available in Africa, Asia, the Caribbean, the US, Europe, Latin America, and the Pacific Islands. Volunteers are of all ages and come from all backgrounds and occupations, including teachers, carpenters, homemakers, physicians, and artists. No special skills or languages are required. Tax-deductible program fees range from $650 to $2,395 and include costs of training, ground transportation, lodging, project materials, all meals, and an experienced team leader. Global Volunteers has recently been designated as a nongovernmental organization in special consultative status with the United Nations Economic and Social Council.

Habitat International Coalition–Housing and Land Rights Network

B-28 Nizamuddin East, New Delhi 110013, India
Tel/Fax: 011 (91 11) 2435-8492
E-mail: hichlrc@vsnl.com
Website: www.hic-mena.org
Contact: Mr. Miloon Kothari or Ms. Shivani Bhardwaj

Habitat International Coalition (HIC) is committed to the recognition, defense, and realization of all peoples' right to a secure place to live in peace and dignity. The Housing and Land Rights Network (HLRN) has offices in Cairo, Geneva, and New Delhi. For more than ten years, HLRN has investigated and documented cases of housing and land rights violations and proposed solutions within the human rights framework. HLRN has taken its analyses to various international bodies, including the UN, to press for better international human rights instruments.

HLRN's office in New Delhi coordinates the South Asian Regional Programme (SARP), working with groups in India, Sri

Lanka, Bhutan, Myanmar, Pakistan, Bangladesh, Tibet, and Nepal. SARP has initiated extensive research on women's rights to housing, land, and property, and children's rights to adequate housing. In addition to programs in South Asia, HLRN–HIC has network members in Mexico, South America, Europe, the Middle East, and Africa. Volunteers must commit to six months or a year and should have prior experience of legal research and excellent writing and coordination skills. Volunteers are expected to cover all costs, although a small stipend may be provided for travel and food expenses. Contact Mr. Miloon Kothari or Ms. Shivani Bhardwaj for more information.

Sudeshna Chatterjee, Volunteer and Research Consultant, Habitat International Coalition

It was a very good experience for me overall, as I got a chance to research, write and advocate human rights instruments, and provide rights-based inputs to local NGOs. The specific research projects that I contributed to were housing rights of women and children in Asia. This experience is proving to be a vital asset for me in my PhD. program in community and environmental design concentration in North Carolina State University in Raleigh. I represented HLRN–HIC as a research consultant in one national and one international conference, where I authored and presented a paper titled "Progressive Realization of the Rights of All Children in Creating Child-Friendly Cities" in the Child in the City conference in Bruges, Belgium, in September 2002.

Hands for Help Nepal

Samakhusi Children Park, PO Box 9012, Kathmandu, Nepal
Tel: 011 (977 1) 981050178 or 011 (977 1) 4362648
Fax: 011 (977 1) 4477018
E-mail: hforh@ntc.net.np
Website: www.handsforhelp.org.np
Contact: Anil Bhusal, director

Hands for Help Nepal is a nonprofit, nongovernmental organization that works throughout Nepal to provide English teaching and training, to raise awareness about environmental, health-care, and gender issues, and to provide training toward economic self-reliance for Nepali people. Volunteers must be at least seventeen years old, and programs last from one to five months in Nepal (five months is the tourist visa limit). The cost is $400 for the first month and $100 for each additional month. Contact the director at the above address for further information.

Incarnate Word Missionaries ◯ R 🐿

4503 Broadway, San Antonio, TX 78230
Tel: (210) 828-2224, ext. 228
Fax: (210) 828-9741
E-mail: iwg017@ccvisanantonio.org
Website: www.incarnatewordsisters.org

Incarnate Word Missionaries (IWM) seeks a new economic, social, and political order that promotes justice and solidarity. Missionaries work with homeless women and children, pastoral ministry, human rights work, teaching, health care, clinic/hospice ministry, and indigenous peoples. Our missionaries serve in the US, Mexico, Guatemala, Peru, and Zambia.

The missionaries must be at least twenty-one years old, of good physical and mental health, single or married with no dependents, willing to commit to one year in their own country or two to three years in a country other than their own, willing to live a simple lifestyle and be open to working with a preferential option for the poor, and of the Christian faith (some sites require that one be Catholic). Those who wish to serve in Latin America must have some degree of fluency in the Spanish language.

The missionary pays the cost of transportation to the orientation site, any language school if needed, vacation travel and emergency leave, and any costs involved for preexisting medical conditions. All other costs are paid by IWM.

International Society for Ecology and Culture

PO Box 9475, Berkeley, CA 94709
Tel: (510) 548-4915
Fax: (510) 548-4916
E-mail: isecca@igc.org
Website: www.isec.org.uk

The International Society for Ecology and Culture (ISEC) is concerned with raising awareness about the root causes of today's social, environmental, and economic crises. Its goals are to challenge economic globalization and conventional notions of "progress" and to promote localization, thereby helping to strengthen community and restore the environment. ISEC produces books, videos, and other educational material and promotes grassroots and policy-level strategies for ecological and community renewal.

One-month farm-stays in ISEC's Ladakh Farm Project are available during July and August. Participants live and work with Ladakhi families in northern India and are exposed to both the strengths of Ladakhi traditional culture and the forces threatening to undermine it. The cost is $350, which includes room and board on the farm. Volunteers are expected to cover their own travel expenses, but financial aid is occasionally available for participants from low-income backgrounds. The Ladakh Farm Project is located at extremely high altitudes and requires a great deal of manual labor, so volunteers should be able to work under these conditions. ISEC does have other volunteer opportunities; contact their office at the above address for more information.

International Volunteer Expeditions

Administrative office: 2001 Vallejo Way, Sacramento, CA 95818
Volunteer Inquiries: PO Box 2071, Roseau, Commonwealth
    of Dominica
Tel: (767) 449-0322
E-mail: ivexinformation@espwa.org
Website: www.espwa.org

International Volunteer Expeditions (IVEX) invites volunteers to assist the endeavors of organizations working for sustainable communities. The programs involve sustainability, poverty, and the environment, including agriculture and biodiversity. The type of work varies, but is primarily physical labor—construction, painting, mapping and surveying, preparing fields for farming, and trail maintenance. Some volunteers with special skills may be assigned such tasks as creating websites, researching and documenting environmental conditions, and planning educational materials. All programs are in partnership with host organizations based in the communities served. Opportunities exist in Mexico, the West Indies, and throughout Central and South America.

Projects ordinarily last one to three weeks. Longer-term placements are available to project alumni. Volunteers pay their own expenses—transportation, incidental expenses, and a registration fee. Costs begin at $475 for six nights, and all expenses are tax-deductible to the extent allowed by law. Accommodations at most project sites are simple, consisting of tents, a dormitory, or the village schoolhouse. English is the working language of all IVEX projects. Technical skills are not required, but a curious, adaptable, and adventurous mind is indispensable.

Interplast

300-B Pioneer Way, Mountain View, CA 94041-1506
Tel: (650) 962-0123
Fax: (650) 962-1619
E-mail: IPNews@interplast.org
Website: www.interplast.org

Interplast is a nonprofit organization partnering with physicians in developing countries to provide free reconstructive plastic surgery for needy children and adults. Interplast coordinates support and advanced training for local surgeons and manages volunteer service programs to care for more than 4,000 impoverished patients every year. Interplast's programs provide surgeries for patients with congenital deformities (cleft lip, cleft palate), or those with severe burns, hand injuries, or other crippling injuries. Interplast's scope of services includes supporting surgeons in developing countries managing their own outreach programs, sending volunteer medical teams overseas to perform the needed surgeries and assist in skills transfer, and conducting workshops providing advanced training in specialized skills for host country medical professionals.

Interplast currently manages medical programs in Bangladesh, Bolivia, Brazil, Ecuador, Honduras, India, Myanmar (Burma), Nepal, Nicaragua, Peru, the Philippines, Sri Lanka, and Vietnam. Plastic surgeons, pediatricians, anesthesiologists, operating room nurses, and recovery room nurses are needed in a volunteer capacity. Placements are generally two weeks. Knowledge of a foreign language is desirable but not required. Each trip participant pays $325 toward travel expenses.

Jesuit Volunteer Corps   R

PO Box 3756, Washington, DC 20027-0256

East Coast:
Tel: (215) 232-0300
E-mail: jvceast@jesuitvolunteers.org

Midwest:
Tel: (313) 345-3480
E-mail: jvcmw@jesuitvolunteers.org

Northwest:
Tel: (503) 335-8202
E-mail: jvcnw@jesuitvolunteers.org

South:
Tel: (713) 756-5095
E-mail: jvcsouth@jesuitvolunteers.org

Southwest:
Tel: (510) 653-8564
E-mail: jvcsw@jesuitvolunteers.org

International:
Tel: (202) 687-1132
E-mail: jvi@jesuitvolunteers.org

Website: www.jesuitvolunteers.org

Each year, Jesuit Volunteer Corps (JVC) offers about 500 men and women the opportunity to work full time for justice and peace by serving the poor directly and working for structural change. The challenge to Jesuit Volunteers (JVs) is to integrate Christian faith by working and living among the poor, living modestly in a cooperative household with other JVs, and examining the causes of social injustice. JVs serve as teachers, counselors, nurses, social workers, community organizers, and lawyers, and work with the homeless, physically and mentally ill, elderly, children, refugees, prisoners, and migrant workers. JVs serve in the US, Belize, Tanzania, Micronesia, Nepal, Peru, Chile, South Africa, Nicaragua, Marshall Islands, Bolivia, and Haiti.

JVC welcomes women and men regardless of economic status, ethnic origin, physical challenge, marital status, or sexual orientation. Applicants must have a Christian motivation, be twenty-one or older, have a college degree or applicable work experience, and be without dependents. There is a particular need for applicants competent in Spanish.

Domestic placements are for one year and begin in August. International placements require a two-year commitment and also begin in August. JVC provides room and board, health insurance, a small personal stipend, local support teams, workshops and retreats during the year, transportation home at the end of term of service, and an active alumni association. Applications are accepted January through July with preference given to applications received before March 1. The deadline for international applicants is February 15.

Emmjolee Mendoza, Volunteer, Jesuit Volunteer Corps

Teacher, St. Peter Claver School, Punta Gorda, Belize

Teaching has been one of the most challenging parts of my experience thus far. My politics and philosophy/pre-law degree did not teach me how to teach the alphabet or how to handle children with various learning disabilities. While I am still an overachiever, I am learning that my work must be looked at from a different perspective. I must not be driven by accomplishment. Success is not the completion of something. And while I am having difficulty teaching my kids how to read, I can offer them something that many others cannot or chose not to give. I can give them my energy, my time, my compassion, and my love. Now, don't get me wrong, this is easy enough to say, but it is probably the most difficult part of the job.

Jewish Volunteer Corps   R ⊕

American Jewish World Service
45 West 36th Street, 10th Floor, New York, NY 10018
Tel: (800) 889-7146 or (212) 736-2597
Fax: (212) 736-3463
E-mail: jvcvol@ajws.org
Website: www.ajws.org

American Jewish World Service is a nonprofit international development agency providing nonsectarian humanitarian assistance to communities throughout the developing world. AJWS works exclusively
with local nongovernmental organizations in the fields of health care,
sustainable agriculture, microcredit, and education. Through the
Jewish Volunteer Corps (JVC), AJWS places professional Jewish men
and women on short-term volunteer consulting assignments with
their partners in the developing world. JVC volunteers provide technical assistance and training to the host organization while experienc-
ing a new country and culture from the inside.

The International Jewish College Corps (IJCC) is a summer program for college students that weaves together an in-depth exploration of international development; study of Jewish texts and
traditions relating to social justice, human rights, religious pluralism,
and racial tolerance; and humanitarian service in hands-on volunteer
projects in the developing world and Israel.

Joint Assistance Center, Inc.

PO Box 6082, San Pablo, CA 94806-0082
Tel: (510) 464-1100
Fax: (510) 217-6671
E-mail: jacusa@juno.com
Website: www.jacusa.org

Joint Assistance Center, Inc. (JAC), is a nongovernmental voluntary
organization headquartered in Haryana State in the outskirts of
Delhi, India. It coordinates conferences and training in various parts
of India on disaster preparedness and works in liaison with groups,
individuals, and small grassroots projects throughout the country,
focusing on such areas as community, welfare, health, education,
youth development, and agricultural training. JAC welcomes volunteers from around the world to participate in the work of its partner
organizations. Short-term projects (minimum one month) can
involve sanitation, construction, agriculture, the environment, public
health, or literacy; long-term projects (three months or more) are
similar to the short-term ones but allow for greater depth.

JAC programs run year-round. Arrangements must be made at
least thirty days in advance of the volunteer's arrival in India.
Volunteers participate in an orientation program in New Delhi before
departing for their assigned village. In New Delhi, volunteers stay at

a JAC-maintained dormitory; accommodations at work camps are in homes, schools, or other public buildings. The registration fee is $50; the cost for one month is $230, airfare not included. For a long-term placement, the fee is $550 for the first three months and $125 for each month thereafter, airfare not included. JAC also coordinates volunteer programs with organizations in Nepal, Bangladesh, and South Korea. Send a self-addressed stamped envelope to the address above, or follow the links from JAC's home page to find out more.

Los Niños

287 G Street, Chula Vista, CA 91910
Tel: (619) 426-9110
Fax: (619) 426-6664
E-mail: info@losninosinternational.org
Website: www.losninosinternational.org

Los Niños supports long-term community development projects in Tijuana, Mexicali, and San Diego. Programs include agriculture, organic gardening, and development education and are designed to promote self-reliance and social awareness. Los Niños offers long-term volunteer opportunities to help assist in these programs. Volunteers are expected to make a minimum commitment of one year. Interested candidates should send a resume to the info e-mail account. Los Niños is not religiously or politically affiliated in any way.

(See listing under Alternative Travel and Study Overseas)

MADRE / Sisters without Borders

121 West 27th Street, Room 301, New York, NY 10001
Tel: (212) 627-0444
Fax (212) 675-3704
E-mail: madre@madre.org
Website: www.madre.org

MADRE places women professionals trained in midwifery; obstetrics; dentistry; nutrition; sexually transmitted disease prevention; reproductive health education; substance abuse counseling; antiviolence training; herbal medicine; trauma counseling; community mental health and health counseling; exercise, massage, and relaxation techniques; child psychology; video production; computers and graphic design; and popular education on health and hygiene in Guatemala, Nicaragua, Chiapas (Mexico), and Palestine. Volunteers provide service and conduct training workshops during short-term residence at MADRE's sister organizations. Volunteers must have credentials and experience in the field in which they would like to work. Knowledge of Spanish is required for Latin America. Volunteers cover their own costs for travel and accommodations. Residencies are for approximately one or two weeks, occasionally longer.

Maryknoll Mission Association of the Faithful R

PO Box 30, Maryknoll, NY 10545-0307
Tel: (800) 818-5276
Fax: (914) 762-7031
E-mail: mmaf@mkl-mmaf.org
Website: www.maryknoll.org

Maryknoll Mission Association of the Faithful, part of the Maryknoll mission family, is a Catholic community of lay, religious, and ordained people, including families and children. Association members participate in the mission of Jesus, working in cross-cultural ministries in order to create a more just world in solidarity with marginalized and oppressed peoples. Missioners come from a wide range of professional and educational backgrounds and may serve in the fields of health (including direct service to persons with AIDS), education, community organizing, grassroots economic development, and formation of faith communities. The association has missions in Kenya, Sudan, Tanzania, Cambodia, Thailand, Vietnam, Bolivia, Brazil, Chile, East Timor, El Salvador, Mexico, Peru, Venezuela, and Zimbabwe.

Mennonite Central Committee R

PO Box 500, Akron, PA 17501-0500
Tel: (717) 859-1151
Fax: (717) 859-2171
E-mail: mailbox@mcc.org
Website: www.mcc.org

Mennonite Central Committee (MCC) is the cooperative relief, service, and development agency of the Mennonite and Brethren in Christ churches in North America. Currently close to 1,400 persons serve in agriculture, health, education, social services, and community development fields in sixty countries, including the US and Canada. Qualifications depend on assignment. Transportation, living expenses, and a small stipend are provided. MCC asks that volunteers be Christian, actively involved in a church congregation, and in agreement with MCC's nonviolent principles. Placements are for three years overseas, two years in North America. For a list of current assignment openings, go to the MCC website.

Middle East Children's Alliance

905 Parker Street, Berkeley, CA 94710
Tel: (510) 548-0542
Fax: (510) 548-0543
E-mail: meca@mecaforpeace.org
Website: www.mecaforpeace.org

The Middle East Children's Alliance (MECA) sponsors Volunteers for Peace in Palestine, a program that places North American volunteers with Palestinian and Israeli NGOs in Jerusalem and the West Bank. Experience in areas such as health, law, agriculture, construction, computers, or English-language tutoring is useful but not required. MECA welcomes anyone who has a genuine concern for and interest in the human rights situation in Palestine and Israel and can maintain a commitment to advocacy and campaign work upon returning to the US. Participants are responsible for covering their own living expenses while abroad, but MECA can help find accommodations or homestays. Internships can vary in length from one to six months.

(See listing under Alternative Travel and Study Overseas)

Mission Volunteers

R

Mission Service Recruitment Office
Presbyterian Church (USA)
100 Witherspoon Street, Louisville, KY 40202
Tel: (888) 728-7228, ext. 2530
Website: www.pcusa.org/msr

The Young Adult Volunteer Program of the Presbyterian Church (USA) is an opportunity for persons between the ages of nineteen and thirty to explore their call to the work of Jesus Christ. This one-year program is an opportunity to experience both mission service and mission learning. Each program site shares common components that enhance the participants' experience: orientation, service, prayer, Bible study and spiritual development, and an end-of-term reentry conference. While sharing these program elements, each site uniquely challenges the participants to explore their relationship to the church and their ministry in a broken world.

Possible sites may include Argentina, Egypt, Ghana, Guatemala, Hungary, southern India, Kenya, Northern Ireland, the Philippines, Thailand, the Ukraine, the United Kingdom, Uruguay, Southeast Alaska, Hollywood (California), Cincinnati (Ohio), Miami (Florida), Nashville (Tennessee), Seattle (Washington), Tucson (Arizona), and West Yellowstone (Montana).

The preferential application deadline is February 1 for service beginning in August and September of the same year. Funding for the year is shared by the Presbyterian Church (USA), supporting congregations or presbyteries and the volunteer. Partial payment of outstanding student loans is available.

The Network in Solidarity with the People of Guatemala

The Guatemala Accompaniment Project
1830 Connecticut Avenue NW, Washington, DC 20009
Tel: (202) 265-8713
Fax: (202) 223-8221
E-mail: nisguagap@igc.org
Website: www.nisgua.org
Contact: Jennifer Morley, US program coordinator,
Guatemala Accompaniment Project

The Network in Solidarity with the People of Guatemala's (NISGUA) Guatemala Accompaniment Project (GAP) creates a nonviolent response to the threats, harassment, and violence suffered by Guatemalan communities and grassroots organizations. To this end, GAP places US volunteers to live side-by-side with at-risk communities and organizations in an effort to deter human rights violations. These volunteers, known as accompaniers, monitor the situation and alert the international community to abuses. The accompanier's presence provides a measure of security and creates space for Guatemalan communities and organizations to organize and defend their rights. Volunteers must commit to at least six months of service, be twenty-one years old, be a US or Canadian citizen, and have proficiency in Spanish. Estimated expenses are $520 to $2,270, although NISGUA provides opportunities for fundraising. Accompaniers receive a stipend, and other related costs are covered (see website for detailed breakdown).

Kareen Erbe, Volunteer, Network in Solidarity with the People of Guatemala

I volunteered as a human rights observer for eight months on the southern coast of Guatemala. I was living and working with a Guatemalan indigenous community that had been internally displaced during Guatemala's thirty-six-year civil war. This was one of the hardest but most transforming experiences of my life. The insight I gained about the nature of resistance, survival, discrimination, poverty, injustice, and reconciliation will stay with me for the rest of my life. In light of the deteriorating human rights situation in Guatemala, the commitment to be a human rights observer in Guatemala should not be taken lightly. Potential volunteers want to weigh the implications of committing to this assignment in terms of the physical and emotional toll this type of work demands. Despite the risks involved, volunteering with NISGUA is a very worthwhile experience, a chance to meet exceptional people, and an opportunity to contribute to meaningful work.

Nicaragua Network

1247 E Street SE, Washington, DC 20003
Tel: (202) 544-9355
Fax: (202) 544-9359
E-mail: nicanet@afgj.org
Website: www.nicanet.org

The Nicaragua Network advocates for sound US foreign policies toward Nicaragua and provides information and organizing tools to a network of 200 solidarity and peace and justice committees across the United States. The network organizes volunteer brigades to assist in the areas of health, construction, or the environment. Two of the most important current areas of solidarity support are labor organizing in the Free Trade Zone of Managua and aid to the efforts of Nicaraguan environmental organizations.

(See listing under Alternative Travel and Study Overseas)

Nuestros Pequeños Hermanos

Apdo. Postal 333, 62000 Cuernavaca, Morelos, Mexi
Tel: 011 (52) 777-311-2654
Fax: 011 (52) 777-311-2655
E-mail: nphint@infosel.net.mx
Website: www.nphamigos.org

Nuestros Pequeños Hermanos (NPH) provides homes for orphaned and abandoned children in Mexico, Honduras, Haiti, Nicaragua, Guatemala, Belize, El Salvador, and the Dominican Republic. The mission is to provide shelter, food, clothing, health care, and education in a Christian family environment based on unconditional acceptance and love. Volunteers should be at least twenty-one years old, with a working knowledge of Spanish (French or Creole for Haiti) and experience working with children. Volunteers must commit to one year of service. Room and board are provided, as well as a small stipend in most countries.

Ron Hicks, Volunteer, Nuestros Pequeños Hermanos

There is not a lot of hand-holding in this volunteer experience. The most successful volunteers have "self-starter" personalities. However, there are plenty of willing and capable people there to learn from and serve as excellent mentors.

The best aspect was feeling that I was doing something tangible to make this world a better place.

You are going to encounter good and bad things there, like in any organization. If you go with the attitude that you are going to change what you consider to be bad in the organization, you will have a disappointing and frustrating experience. However, if you go with an open mind and your primary desire is to serve and love the children, you can be guaranteed an amazing and life-changing experience.

Operation Crossroads Africa

34 Mount Morris Park West, New York, NY 10027
Tel: (211) 289-1949
Fax: (212) 289-2526
E-mail: oca@igc.org
Website: www.igc.org/oca

Established in 1957, Operation Crossroads Africa oversees two volunteer programs: the Africa program, which annually supports fifteen to twenty work projects in Africa, and the Diaspora program, which focuses on Brazil because of its large Afro-Brazilian population. Crossroads programs run in the following African countries: Benin, Botswana, Burkina Faso, Ethiopia, the Gambia, Ghana, Kenya, Lesotho, Malawi, Mali, Namibia, Senegal, South Africa, Tanzania, and Uganda. The Crossroads summer consists of three orientation days in New York City, six weeks of service on a rural project, and one week of travel in the host country. All Crossroads ventures are community initiated, and volunteers live and work with hosts who have designed the project. Among the possible assignments are construction of community facilities, public health drives, reforestation, and teaching. Specialized skills in medicine, construction, or local languages are welcome but not necessary. The fee for participation is $3,500 exclusive of transportation to and from New York. Crossroads provides fundraising advice and a limited number of partial scholarships based on need. Successful participation requires an interest in Africa and the Diaspora, strong communication skills, a desire to establish meaningful contact with people of other cultures, and a willingness to respect different beliefs and values. Many volunteers have been able to arrange academic credit for their service with Crossroads.

Peace Brigades International

428 8th Street SE, Washington, DC 20003
Tel: (202) 544-3765
Fax: (202) 544-3766
E-mail: andrew@pbiusa.org
Website: www.peacebrigades.org

Founded in 1981, Peace Brigades International (PBI) pioneered and practices an effective approach to human rights protection known as protective accompaniment. PBI fields teams of international volunteers trained in nonviolence to accompany individuals and organizations facing death threats as a result of their work on behalf of human rights and social justice. PBI's work—based on the principals of nonviolence, nonpartisanship, and noninterference in the affairs of the groups we accompany—also includes intensive networking with local, national, and international officials; distribution of human rights information to the international community; and public education in the US and other countries.

PBI currently has projects in Colombia, Guatemala, Indonesia, and Mexico. Prospective volunteers attend a seven- to ten-day training before final selections are made. Participants must be at least twenty-five years old and willing to commit to one year of field service. Candidates for our Latin America projects must be fluent in Spanish, and candidates for Indonesia must be conversant in or willing to learn Bahasa Indonesian. Upon acceptance PBI covers travel, housing, food, health insurance, and other work-related expenses, in addition to a modest monthly stipend.

Peacework

209 Otey Street, Blacksburg, VA 24060-7426
Tel: (540) 953-1376
Fax: (540) 953-0300
E-mail: mail@peacework.org
Website: www.peacework.org

Peacework manages short-term volunteer service projects around the world in cooperation with indigenous relief and development organizations. Projects are normally organized with groups and can be arranged for college, university, and community service organizations. Orientation and interaction with the host community is a vital part of the program, in addition to the assistance which volunteers provide in building houses, schools, and health facilities, as well as school tutoring, agriculture, and other projects with a local community focus. Peacework also has a medical program for health-care professionals. International experience, building skills, volunteer service, and foreign language proficiency are helpful but not required. Anyone with a genuine interest in global service is invited to participate. Project locations change each year and have been offered in places such as Vietnam, Russia, Mexico, the Czech Republic, Honduras, the Dominican Republic, Belize, Nicaragua, Costa Rica, and the United States. Typical costs range from $500 to $1,000 plus airfare. Limited scholarships are available. Contact Peacework for information about annual projects, dates, and costs.

Plenty International

PO Box 394, Summertown, TN 38483
Tel/Fax: (931) 964-4864
E-mail: plenty@plenty.org
Website: www.plenty.org

Founded in 1974, Plenty promotes the exchange of appropriate village-scale technologies, skills, and resources between people worldwide in a spirit of cooperation and friendship. Special focus is on projects to assist indigenous peoples. Plenty can only manage a small number of volunteers per year. Projects utilizing volunteers are based primarily in Belize. Volunteers must pay their own travel and living expenses. Long-term volunteers (three months or more) with specific skills in organic agriculture, midwifery, or sustainable energy are needed. Check the website for a listing of current volunteer opportunities.

Quest   R

3706 Rhode Island Avenue, Mt. Rainier, MD 20712
Tel: (301) 277-3594
E-mail: Joanfaraone@aol.com
Website: www.quest-rjm.org

Quest, a volunteer program sponsored by the Religious of Jesus and Mary, offers year-long and summer opportunities in Gros Morne and Jean Rabel, Haiti. Volunteers share simple living in Christian community while daily serving the poor in a variety of social and educational ministries. Orientation, room, board, medical insurance, monthly stipend, retreats, and daily transportation are provided. Volunteers must provide their own transportation at the beginning and end of the term.

Service Civil International–International Voluntary Service

US Branch of Service Civil International
5474 Walnut Level Road, Crozet, VA 22932
Tel/Fax: (206) 530-6585
E-mail: sciinfo@sci-ivs.org
Website: www.sci-ivs.org

Service Civil International (SCI) organizes work camps in the US, Latin America, Europe, Asia, and Africa to promote cross-cultural understanding and international peace. Volunteers work on environmental, construction, solidarity, and social service projects and live together in simple quarters for two to four weeks. Volunteers must be sixteen or older for US work camps, eighteen or older for camps in developed nations, and at least twenty-one with SCI work camp experience for projects in developing nations. Volunteers pay travel expenses; SCI covers room, board, and accident insurance. Some partners in developing counties charge an extra fee. Many work camps are accessible to disabled people. SCI-IVS application fees are $175 for overseas and $115 for US camps.

Toledo Eco-Tourism Association and Punta Gorda Conservation Committee

PO Box 45, Punta Gorda, Belize
Tel: 011 (501 7) 22119
E-mail: ttea@btl.net

The Toledo Eco-Tourism Association (TEA) works with fourteen indigenous communities (thirteen Maya and one Garifuna) in the areas of eco-tourism, rain forest conservation, and sustainable development. The association has been active since 1990. Founded in 1996, the Punta Gorda Conservation Committee (PGCC) is an urban group seeking to establish eco-tourist sites on what remains of the public land around Punta Gorda. The sites will be run by and for the benefit of local people. Volunteers have worked as instructors in training for office operation, trail development, guide training, arts and crafts development, grant writing, and media. A major current project is the establishment of community conservation areas for nineteen villages for which a grant is pending with UNDP. Volunteers must cover all expenses, including transportation, room, and board, at an average of $20 per day or $400 per month. Belizeans speak English. Volunteers should commit to a stay of three to six months.

Visions in Action

2710 Ontario Road NW, Washington, DC 20009
Tel: (202) 625-7402
E-mail: visions@igc.org
Website: www.visionsinaction.org

Visions in Action is a nonprofit organization that offers six-month and one-year volunteer positions in four African countries and Mexico. Positions are available with nonprofit development organizations, research institutes, health clinics, community groups, and the media. The program features a month-long orientation, including intensive language study, followed by a five- or eleven-month volunteer placement. All countries have one-year programs; the six-month option is possible in South Africa, Uganda, and Mexico. Visions in Action also offers short-term programs in Mexico and Tanzania: a seven-week summer program and a three-week winter program ideal for those seeking a short-term volunteer placement. Volunteers for long-term programs must be at least twenty years of age, and have two years of college or equivalent work experience. Most volunteers are university graduates; the average age is twenty-seven. The program is open to people of any nationality. Married couples are encouraged to apply as well. The minimum age for the short-term programs is eighteen. Program fees cover housing, health insurance, medical evacuation insurance, orientation, local staff and in-country support, program administration, and stipend. Program fees vary by country. The average cost is $4,000.

Voluntarios Solidarios
Fellowship of Reconciliation

Task Force on Latin America and the Caribbean
2017 Mission Street, #305, San Francisco, CA 94110
Tel: (415) 495-6334
Fax: (415) 495-5628
E-mail: volfor@igc.org
Website: www.forusa.org

Voluntarios Solidarios places volunteers with Latin American and Caribbean groups engaged in nonviolence education, human rights documentation, and advocacy efforts with the regions' poor majority. Each volunteer's work is shaped by the needs of the host organization. Common needs include translation of publications, support of peace actions, technical assistance in carpentry, computer operation, recycling, assistance with human welfare service, child and elderly care projects, and conflict resolution. Volunteers must be self-funded, at least twenty-one years old, and functional in Spanish. Lengths of placements range from three months to two years.

Volunteers for Peace, Inc.

1034 Tiffany Road, Belmont, VT 05730
Tel: (802) 259-2759
Fax: (802) 259-2922
E-mail: vfp@vfp.org
Website: www.vfp.org

Volunteers for Peace (VFP) recruits volunteers for over 2,000 work camps in eighty different countries. At a work camp, ten to twenty people from five or more countries join together for two to three weeks to support community projects in construction, restoration, environmental work, social services, agriculture, and archaeology. In 2002, VFP exchanged over 1,300 volunteers. Volunteers arrange their own travel and pay a registration fee of $200, which covers room and board for the duration of most programs. Volunteers can participate in multiple camps in the same or different countries. Call, write, or e-mail VFP for a free newsletter, which includes many reports and photos from their programs.

Volunteers in Asia

PO Box 20266, Stanford, CA 94309
Tel: (650) 723-3228
Fax: (650) 725-1805
E-mail: info@viaprograms.org
Website: www.viaprograms.org

At the request of Asian institutions, Volunteers in Asia (VIA) places undergraduates and recent graduates in teaching and English resource positions in China, Indonesia, and Vietnam. Applicants must attend a weeklong predeparture training program at Stanford University in July. Volunteers pay an initial fee of $1,975 for a one-year placement or $975 for a two-year placement. This fee covers insurance, training costs, and roundtrip airfare. The host institution provides an in-country stipend for basic living expenses and housing.

Witness for Peace

1229 15th Street NW, Washington, DC 20005
Tel: (202) 588-1471
Fax: (202) 588-1472
E-mail: witness@witnessforpeace.org
Website: www.witnessforpeace.org

Volunteers with Witness for Peace (WFP) work with communities in Nicaragua, Mexico, Colombia, and Cuba, making a two-year commitment. Long-term volunteers document human rights abuses, study the effects of North American foreign and economic policies on the region, provide sociopolitical analyses of domestic affairs, facilitate short-term delegations of North Americans, and stand with the people in the spirit of international awareness and the ethos of nonviolence as a means for positive social change. Volunteers must be US citizens and fluent in Spanish. Volunteers pay costs of roundtrip airfare and attempt to raise $1,000 for WFP to help cover living expenses. WFP provides training, room and board, medical, and a monthly stipend. WPF is an interfaith organization.

Andrew Schwiebert, Volunteer, Witness for Peace

What began for me as an apprehensive two-year commitment to live and work abroad grew to become an incredibly transformative, intense, and fulfilling three-year adventure in Mexico, Guatemala, Nicaragua, and Colombia. Some of the highlights of my experience with Witness for Peace were educating and training hundreds of human rights activists from the US, providing international accompaniment to threatened human rights leaders and their communities, deepening my grasp of a foreign language, traveling extensively throughout the Americas, writing grassroots education reports, and speaking to members of Congress in Washington, DC. I had the incredible opportunity to be a part of building a grassroots movement to make US foreign policy more just and sustainable toward the developing world, made friends for life in a community-living environment, and developed important skills that prepare me for varied career paths in the fields of international policy change, human rights, international development, or faith-based social change, among others. My life has been changed, and I am fundamentally a different, better person because of the connection I made to Witness for Peace through *Alternatives to the Peace Corps*.

WorkingAbroad Projects

2nd Floor Office Suite, 59, Lansdowne Place, Hove, East Sussex, BN3 1FL, England
Tel/Fax: 011 (44 0) 1273-711-406
E-mail: info@workingabroad.com
Website: www.workingabroad.com

WorkingAbroad Projects provides volunteer assistance to small-scale organizations on request. Projects usually focus on cultural development, earth restoration, permaculture, indigenous rights, or traditional arts and music. Currently, WorkingAbroad Projects has programs in the Netherlands Antilles and in Costa Rica. Volunteers should be at least eighteen years old and culturally aware. The cost for the two-month program ranges from $859 to $1,480, which includes room and board, materials, training, and local transportation.

WorldTeach, Inc.

Center for International Development
Harvard University
79 John F. Kennedy Street, Cambridge, MA 02138
Tel: (800) 483-2240 or (617) 495-5527
Fax: (617) 495-1599
E-mail: info@worldteach.org
Website: www.worldteach.org

WorldTeach is a private, nonprofit organization based at the Center for International Development at Harvard University. Founded in 1986, WorldTeach provides opportunities for individuals to make a meaningful contribution to international education while living and working as volunteer teachers in developing countries. Volunteers teach English for two to twelve months to students of a variety of ages, depending on the country. Currently, teachers are needed in Costa Rica, China, Ecuador, Namibia, the Yucatán, and Marshall Islands. A bachelor's degree is required for long-term teaching assignments. Some summer assignments are available, which are open to all individuals eighteen years of age or older. No previous language or teaching experience is necessary.

Housing is provided during the period of service, and volunteers pay a fee covering direct expenses such as international airfare, insurance, training and orientation, room and board, and in-country staff support. Volunteers receive a small monthly living allowance during the course of their service. Student loans may be deferred while volunteers serve. Applications are accepted on a rolling admissions basis and may be printed from the WorldTeach website or requested by contacting the WorldTeach admissions office.

Key to Icons

See page 29 for full description.

R   Religious affiliation.

◯   Foreign language proficiency requested.

◔   Short-term volunteer opportunities available.

💵   Financial assistance available.

US Voluntary Service Organizations

Working overseas is not the only way to gain community development experience. In many areas of the US, people face conditions of poverty similar to those found in other countries. Voluntary service in the US can offer a low-cost opportunity for building solid credentials toward a career in community development.

One of the best resources for domestic volunteering may well be your local Yellow Pages, under Social Service Organizations. Here are some organizations that recruit nationally and perform admirable work.

Association of Community Organizations for Reform Now

88 Third Avenue, Brooklyn, NY 11217
Tel: (718) 246-7900
Fax: (718) 246-7939
E-mail: fielddirect@acorn.org
Website: www.acorn.org

Association of Community Organizations for Reform Now (ACORN) is a neighborhood-based, multiracial membership organization of low-income families working to gain power within institutions that affect their everyday lives. Volunteers work as grassroots organizers throughout the US. They receive a salary and must commit to one year of service. A working knowledge of Spanish and previous organizing experience are preferred, but not required.

Bikes Not Bombs

59 Amory Street, Suite103, Roxbury, MA 02119
Tel: (617) 442-0004
Fax: (617) 445-2439
E-mail: mail@bikesnotbombs.org
Website: www.bikesnotbombs.org

Bikes Not Bombs (BNB) is a nonprofit grassroots development and solidarity organization that uses bicycles for development work overseas and also for youth programs and community environmental action in the Boston area. In other countries, BNB helps local groups form ecologically viable bicycle workshops and related projects in Central America, the Caribbean, and Africa. These projects have involved the collecting of over 20,000 donated bicycles and tons of parts from across the US, recycling them to Nicaragua, Haiti, the Dominican Republic, El Salvador, Guatemala, and Ghana. BNB provides technical assistance, training, tools, and occasionally financing for these projects. In the Boston area, BNB runs many youth programs, including Earn-A-Bike, in which youth learn mechanics and riding skills and rebuild a bicycle to be their own. Youth job training and paid work are available in the full-service bike shop. Interns can work in Boston with youth programs, event planning, transportation and environmental activism, bike mechanics, or computer and web issues. Experienced bilingual mechanics and personnel are very occasionally placed overseas to carry out fieldwork.

Buddhist Alliance for Social Engagement   R

PO Box 4650, Berkeley, CA 94704
Tel: (415) 643-8289
Fax: (510) 655-1369
E-mail: base@bpf.org
Website: www.bpf.org/base.html

Buddhist Alliance for Social Engagement (BASE) is a program of the Buddhist Peace Fellowship, begun in the San Francisco Bay Area in 1995. BASE provides a structure for a group of volunteers to spend six months in service/social change work combined with intensive Buddhist practice. Placements include work in soup kitchens, shelters, hospices, urban community garden projects, and social justice organizations. Those volunteering thirty hours a week are offered a modest stipend and housing.

BASE volunteers meet regularly for study of Engaged Buddhism, meditation, and discussion and support. Applicants must have service, group, and meditation experience. In addition to Bay Area BASE groups, the program has expanded to include groups in Boston, Massachusetts; Boulder, Colorado; and Santa Cruz and Arcata, California.

Casa de Proyecto Libertad

113 North First Street, Harlingen, TX 78550
Tel: (956) 425-9552
Fax: (956) 425-8249

Casa de Proyecto Libertad (PL) promotes and defends the human rights of the border communities in South Texas through immigration legal services, advocacy, and community organizing. PL's legal programs include representation in immigration court and with the INS, NACARA Project, Unaccompanied Minors in Detention Project, Violence Against Women Act (VAWA) Project, as well as working with Political Asylum, Temporary Protected Status, Naturalization, and Family Visa Applicants. PL also facilitates the emergence of grassroots community organizations whose members are impacted by immigration laws and enforcement policies. PL provides human rights trainings as one step toward self-determination and social change. There are volunteer opportunities in the legal and community organizing programs. Must speak Spanish and be conscious of cultural differences. Volunteers pay their own expenses, but some assistance may be available.

Catholic Worker Movement   R

The Catholic Worker
36 East First Street, New York, NY 10003
Website: www.catholicworker.org

The Catholic Worker Movement has165 locations throughout the US and Canada, as well as 16 international locations; for a copy of or subscription to the *Catholic Worker* newspaper, contact the address above. Founded by Dorothy Day and Peter Maurin in 1933, the Catholic Worker Movement is grounded in the firm belief of the God-given dignity of every person. CW communities are committed to nonviolence, voluntary poverty, and hospitality for the homeless, exiled, hungry, and forsaken. Houses are independent of one another and vary in their activities, relationship to the Catholic Church, and how they incorporate Catholic Worker philosophy and tradition. Most are based on the Gospel, prayer, and Catholic beliefs, but some are interfaith. There is no national Catholic Worker headquarters. Catholic Workers live a simple lifestyle in community, serve the poor, and resist war and social injustice. Most houses need volunteers; contact the house you are interested in directly for further information. The national CW website maintains a complete list of community houses.

Center for Third World Organizing

1218 East 21st Street, Oakland, CA 94606
Tel: (510) 533-7583
Fax: (510) 533-0923
E-mail: training@ctwo.org
Website: www.ctwo.org

The Center for Third World Organizing (CTWO) is a research and training center working on issues affecting third world communities throughout the United States. Its Minority Activists Apprenticeship Program (MAAP) provides training and field experience for young people of color who are involved in working for social justice. Community Action Training (CAT) is conducted in the spring, prior to the seven-week MAAP internship program, which trains people (primarily college students) in the techniques of community organizing. Volunteers receive housing and a stipend. Other internships are sometimes available including research and writing for partnership programs.

Citizen Action of New York

94 Central Avenue, Albany, NY 12206
Tel: (518) 465-4600, ext. 109
Fax: (518) 465-2890
E-mail: mail@citizenactionny.org or nmerrill@citizenactionny.org
Website: www.citizenactionny.org
Contact: Nicole Merrill, communications associate

Citizen Action of New York (a state affiliate of US Action) works at the grassroots level for social, economic, racial, and environmental justice across New York state. Volunteers work on one of the four current issue campaigns (Education, After-School, Health Care, or Clean Money/Clean Elections) in one of the five state offices, located in Buffalo, Binghamton, Long Island, Brooklyn, and Albany.

Volunteers usually work with Citizen Action for a semester or a summer and are required to have some knowledge of American government. Interns and volunteers are expected to pay all living and transportation expenses. Paid internship opportunities occasionally arise based on foundation or grant support and are posted on the website regularly. Contact the communications associate at nmerrill@citizenactionny.org or at the phone number above.

Council for Responsible Genetics

5 Upland Drive, Suite 3, Cambridge, MA 02140
Tel: (617) 868-0870
Fax: (617) 491-5344
E-mail: crg@gene-watch.org
Website: www.gene-watch.org

The Council for Responsible Genetics (CRG) is a nonprofit organization fostering public debate about the social, ethical, and environmental implications of genetic technologies. CRG works through the media and concerned citizens to distribute accurate information and represent the public interest on emerging issues in biotechnology. CRG's primary program areas include genetic privacy and discrimination, biological warfare, genetically modified foods, human genetic modification, and reproductive technologies.

Four core principles drive the organization's work:

1. The public must have access to clear and understandable information on technological innovations.

2. The public must be able to participate in public and private decision making concerning technological developments and their implementation.

3. New technologies must meet social needs.

4. Problems rooted in poverty, racism, and other forms of inequality cannot be remedied by technology alone.

Unpaid internships are available during the summer and during the academic year. Interns should be qualified undergraduate and graduate students interested in bioethics and emerging biotechnologies. Opportunities include working with senior staff and board members on individual research, writing, or outreach projects in specific program areas. Interns should submit application materials to Peter Shorett.

Episcopal Urban Internship Program R

260 North Locust Street, Inglewood, CA 90301
Tel: (310) 771-0660
Fax: (310) 771-0634
E-mail: euip@pacbell.net
Website: www.euip.org

The Episcopal Urban Internship Program is a one-year voluntary service program for young adults (ages twenty-one to thirty). Interns are placed with urban social service organizations within the Los Angeles area and live communally in a house in Inglewood. In addition to their job placements, the interns are expected to play an active role in their household community, spiritual activities, and to take part in the life of the sponsoring Episcopal parish. Individuals do not need to be Episcopalians to be urban interns. The program provides a monthly stipend, along with health insurance and housing. Participants are eligible for an AmeriCorps grant upon completion of the year. Additional benefits include quarterly retreats and weekly theological reflection times.

Food First/Institute for Food and Development Policy

(See description of Food First at the back of this book)

The Food Project

Box 705, Lincoln, MA 01773
Tel: (781) 259-8621
Fax: (781) 259-9659
E-mail: cwatts@thefoodproject.org
Website: www.thefoodproject.org

The Food Project's mission is to create a thoughtful and productive community of youth and adults from diverse backgrounds who work together to build a sustainable food system. The Food Project's organic farms in Boston and Lincoln produce healthy food for city and suburb residents in the surrounding area. Volunteers help on both farms from April through June and from September through mid-November. Volunteers work from one to three days per week to full time through the growing season. No previous farming experience is required. Volunteers must be at least fifteen years of age. Occasionally there are volunteer opportunities in the kitchen or with other programs.

Heifer International
315 West Ponce de Leon Avenue, Suite 245, Decatur, GA 30030
Tel: (404) 687-0194
Fax: (404) 373-5508
E-mail: info@heifer.org
Website: www.heifer.org
Contact: Leslie Withers, national volunteer coordinator

Heifer Project International has helped more than four million impoverished families worldwide become more self-reliant through the gift of livestock and training in their care. Heifer has two kinds of volunteer opportunities. Community volunteers work in their own communities to educate people about world hunger and Heifer's innovative solutions, raise money for Heifer's work, staff display booths at conference and conventions, or help out in one of ten regional offices. For details, contact Leslie Withers, national volunteer coordinator, at the above address or by e-mail at leslie.withers@heifer.org. Residential volunteer opportunities are available for people with the following interests or skills: general farm/livestock workers, construction, hospitality, cafeteria, office work, speakers, media volunteers, educational staff, organic gardening, or agro-forestry. These activities take place at one of three Learning Centers, located in Perryville, AR, Rutland, MA, and Ceres, CA. Learning Center volunteers are provided a small stipend, food, and housing. For more information, contact: Learning Center Volunteer Manager, 55 Heifer Road, Perryville, AR 72126; 501-889-5124; e-mail: ranchvol@heifer.org.

(See listing under Alternative Travel and Study Overseas)

Indigenous Tourism Rights International
366 North Prior Avenue, Suite 205, Saint Paul, MN 55104
Tel: (651) 644-9984
E-mail: info@tourismrights.org
Website: www.tourismrights.org

Indigenous Tourism Rights International (formerly the Rethinking Tourism Project) was established in 1995 as an indigenous people's organization dedicated to collaborating with indigenous communities and networks to help protect native territories, rights, and cultures. Their mission is to facilitate the exchange of local experiences in order for indigenous peoples to understand, challenge, and take control of the ways in which tourism affects our lives. Tourism Rights works with indigenous communities to develop critical education materials and technical assistance on a wide range of tourism-related subjects—human rights, displacement, migration, policy, education, and others.

Tourism Rights offers three internships per semester (fall, spring, and summer), for three months at eight to fifteen hours per week. These are nonpaid positions and are in their Saint Paul, Minnesota, office. Interns' projects may include communications and networking, fundraising, publication and graphic design, or translation. Interns should be independent, self-motivated, and interested in environmental or international issues. Spanish language interpretation/ translation skills are extremely helpful.

Lutheran Volunteer Corps

1226 Vermont Avenue NW, Washington, DC 20005
Tel: (202) 387-3222
Fax: (202) 667-0037
E-mail: lvcrecruitment@lvchome.org
Website: www.lvchome.org

Lutheran Volunteer Corps volunteers work in advocacy and public policy, AIDS/HIV, community development and organizing, education, the environment, food and hunger, health care, housing, immigration and refugee services, legal assistance, social and direct services, shelters, and programs for women and youth. Placements are in Baltimore, MD; Wilmington, DE; Washington, DC; Chicago, IL; Milwaukee, WI; Minneapolis/St. Paul, MN; Seattle and Tacoma, WA; and Oakland/Berkeley, CA. Volunteers live communally with three to six other volunteers, commit to living a simplified lifestyle, and work for social justice. Travel, room and board, medical coverage, and daily work-related transportation expenses are covered. The program is open to people of all faiths and ages. Married couples and couples in committed partnerships are welcome to apply. LVC is a

Reconciling in Christ Organization. Contact the Recruitment Coordinator.

Mennonite Voluntary Service

PO Box 347, 722 Main Street, Newton, KS 67117-0347
E-mail: service@MennoniteMission.net
Website: www.service.MennoniteMission.net

Mennonite Voluntary Service (MVS) helps meet the needs of poor and disadvantaged people in the US and Canada. Volunteer placements range from staffing food banks and emergency assistance centers to working with after school programs. Social work, community organization, housing rehabilitation, and education skills are in particular demand. Initial terms of two years are strongly encouraged, though some assignments are also available for one year. Spanish is helpful or required for some positions. Volunteers must be Christian, at least twenty years old, and from the US or Canada. All expenses are covered by MVS.

National Coalition for the Homeless

1012 14th Street NW, Suite 600, Washington, DC 20005-3471
Tel: (202) 737-6444, ext. 19
Fax: (202) 737-6445
E-mail: mstoops@nationalhomeless.org
Website: www.nationalhomeless.org
Contact: Michael Stoops, director of community organizing

The National Coalition for the Homeless (NCH) works to create the systematic and attitudinal changes necessary to prevent and end homelessness through grassroots organizing, public education, policy advocacy, and technical assistance. NCH also works to meet the immediate needs of those who are homeless or at risk of becoming homeless and takes as its first principle of practice to involve those who have experienced homelessness to be involved in all aspects of the organization's work.

Each year NCH offers a limited number of volunteer/internship opportunities. Generally volunteers/interns are assigned to one of the issue areas of NCH's work: civil rights, health, affordable housing, income, media/publications, and grassroots organizing. Positions last from three weeks to a year. Many of NCH's volunteers/interns are currently undergraduate or graduate students or have recently graduated. However, others are encouraged to apply. Volunteers/interns are expected to pay for their own expenses, although students may want to check with their universities about receiving school credit or a stipend. NCH volunteers also include a speaker's bureau coordinator and development coordinator through the AmeriCorps VISTA program, through which they serve for one year and receive a stipend.

Pesticide Action Network North America

49 Powell Street, Suite 500, San Francisco, CA 94102
Tel: (415) 981-1771
Fax: (415) 981-1991
E-mail: angelica@panna.org or skegley@panna.org
Website: www.panna.org
Contact: Angelica Barrera, office manager

Pesticide Action Network North America (PANNA) works to replace pesticide use with ecologically sound and socially just alternatives. As one of five PAN regional centers worldwide, the San Francisco office links local and international consumer, labor, health, environment, and agriculture groups into an international citizens' action network. This network challenges the global proliferation of pesticides, defends basic rights to health and environmental quality, and works to insure the transition to a just and viable society. PANNA accepts volunteers on a year-round basis. Projects and length of time vary depending on the program's needs.

Sioux Indian YMCA

PO Box 218, Dupree, SD 57623
Tel: (605) 365-5232
Fax: (605) 365-5230
E-mail: info@siouxymca.org
Website: www.siouxymca.org

The Sioux YMCA is the only YMCA in the US on an Indian reservation. Located on the Cheyenne River Sioux Reservation, the organization mostly serves Lakota Sioux families. The YMCA offers two types of volunteer opportunities to college age or older volunteers. Volunteers can serve for two months during the summer as camp staff at YMCA Camp Leslie Marrowbone, working with seven- to fourteen-year-old children. Also needed are community development volunteers to live in Dupree and support various youth and family programs. These placements are three to twelve months. Volunteers must have camp or community work skills, and be flexible and open to a new culture. Both positions provide housing and a stipend.

United Farm Workers of America

PO Box 62 La Paz, Keene, CA 93531
Tel: (661) 823-6250
Fax: (661) 823-6177
E-mail: fwmrecruiter@hotmail.com
Website: www.ufw.org

United Farm Workers (UFW) works for justice for farmworkers and safe food for consumers. UFW is seeking staff to organize farmworkers and consumers. They offer competitive salaries depending on experience and benefits.

Key to Icons

See page 29 for full description.

R Religious affiliation.

 Foreign language proficiency requested.

Short-term volunteer opportunities available.

Financial assistance available.

Alternative Travel and Study Overseas

In this section you will find shorter-term volunteer opportunities as well as options for travel to unusual destinations. A brief work stint with one of the organizations listed here (say a two-week excursion building a well in Nicaragua with El Porvenir) can acquaint you with living in poor countries and help you decide if a long-term commitment makes sense for you. A number of groups conduct "reality tours," study tours, or delegations in developing countries and the US. These are socially responsible educational tours that provide participants with firsthand experience of the political, economic, and social structures that create or sustain hunger, poverty, and environmental degradation. Tour participants meet with people from diverse sectors with various perspectives on issues of agriculture, development, and the environment. They often stay with local people, visit rural areas, and meet with grassroots organizers. The experience and insights gained on such a tour may influence participants' future work for democratic social change. Many universities offer study-abroad programs. This section mentions just a few of these.

African American Studies Program
PO Box 497327, Chicago, IL 60649
Tel: (773) 667-1285
Fax: (773) 684-6967
E-mail: hrogers67@aol.com

The African American Studies Program offers a variety of study tours throughout Africa. Past tour themes have included economic and political development of states and the role of women in the family. Tours are led by scholars of African studies.

Amizade, Ltd.

(See listing under International Voluntary Service Organizations)

Bike-Aid

Global Exchange
2017 Mission Street, Suite 303, San Francisco, CA 94110
Tel: (415) 255-7296 or (800) 743-3808
E-mail: bikeaid@globalexchange.org
Website: www.globalexchange.org

Bike-Aid is an innovative cross-country cycling adventure sponsored by Global Exchange. Global Exchange is a nonprofit human rights organization working for global political, economic, environmental, and social justice. Bike-Aid combines physical challenge, community interaction, global education, leadership, fundraising, and service learning into the empowering experience of a lifetime. Every summer individuals from around the world cycle across the country (starting in San Francisco or Seattle to Washington, DC) and on a shorter two-week California coastal ride to the Mexican border. Along the routes, participants exchange information and get a firsthand look into local community groups, the issues that are facing them, and the solutions that are taking place. Overnight lodging includes organic farms, Native American Indian reservations, churches, and camping in some of the most beautiful spots the US has to offer.

Everyone from beginners to prize-winning racers has participated in Bike-Aid, and riders from the ages of sixteen to sixty have met the challenge. It is not a race, and Global Exchange encourages the participation of people from all backgrounds, ages, and abilities. Cyclists must be willing to live in a community throughout the summer, and intern/volunteers must be resourceful and able to work in a team environment.

Center for Global Education

Augsburg College
2211 Riverside Avenue, Minneapolis, MN 55454
Tel: (800) 299-8889 or (612) 330-1159
Fax: (612) 330-1695
E-mail: globaled@augsburg.edu
Website: www.augsburg.edu

The Center for Global Education designs and coordinates travel seminars to Central America, Mexico, the Caribbean, and southern Africa. The goal is to foster critical analysis of local and global conditions so that personal and systemic change takes place. Participants meet with a wide range of representatives in government and business, church, and grassroots communities. The focus is on sustainable development, human rights, women's roles, and the role and responsibility of people in working for social change. The center's programs are utilized by a wide variety of civic groups, churches, colleges, and individuals. They also arrange longer study programs for undergraduate students.

Christian Peacemaker Teams   R

PO Box 6508, Chicago, IL 60680-6508
Tel: (773) 277-0253
Fax: (773) 277-0291
E-mail: cpt@igc.org
Website: www.cpt.org

Christian Peacemaker Teams (CPT) leads short-term study delegations several times yearly to areas of conflict or heightened militarization. CPT is cross-denominational, with strong roots grounded in the Quakers, Mennonites, and Church of the Brethren.

Study tour participants are self-funded and should be at least eighteen years of age.

(See listing under International Voluntary Service Organizations)

Christians for Peace in El Salvador   R

122 DeWitt Drive, Boston MA 02120
Tel: (617) 445-5115
Fax: (617) 249-0769
E-mail: info@crispaz.org
Website: www.crispaz.org

Founded in 1984, Christians for Peace in El Salvador (CRISPAZ) is a faith-based organization dedicated to mutual accompaniment with the church of the poor and marginalized communities in El Salvador. In building bridges of solidarity between communities in El Salvador and those in their home countries, CRISPAZ volunteers strive together for peace, justice, and human liberation. El Salvador Encounter is a faith-based experience in which participants can learn about current Salvadoran reality. Encounters are seven to ten days long and offer the opportunity to explore a different reality and build relationships with people of a different culture.

(See listing under International Voluntary Organizations)

Co-op America Travel-Links

120 Beacon Street, Somerville, MA 02143
Tel: (800) 648-2667 or (617) 497-8163
Fax: (617) 492-3720
E-mail: mj@tvlcoll.com

Travel-Links is a full-service travel agency that emphasizes responsible tourism and seeks to promote understanding and cooperation among people through nonexploitative travel. Make your travel dollars count.

Cultural Restoration Tourism Project

c/o Mark A. Hintzke
410 Paloma Avenue, Pacifica, CA 94044
Tel: (415) 563-7221
E-mail: info@crtp.net
Website: www.crtp.net

In Mongolia in the summer of 1999, the Cultural Restoration Tourism Project (CRTP) began the restoration of the Baldan Baraivan temple, built in the 1700s, badly damaged in the 1930s by the Soviet regime, and one of the few standing Buddhist monasteries of its kind. Through the use of volunteer tourism, CRTP will fund and execute the restoration of the main temple. Tours are available to the general public each summer through the project's completion, currently scheduled for 2006. Participants do not need any construction experience, just a will and a desire to see the temple rebuilt. Local community members will be employed full time, and participants will work alongside Mongolian staff. Everyone stays in traditional yurts, each of which houses two to three people. Opportunities for overnights in the wilderness will be available; travelers should bring their own tents if interested in camping or desiring private accommodations.

Earthwatch

3 Clock Tower Place, Suite 100, Box 75, Maynard, MA 01754
Tel: (800) 776-0188 or (978) 461-2332
E-mail: info@earthwatch.org
Website: www.earthwatch.org

Earthwatch sponsors scholarly field research using volunteers to help scientists on research expeditions around the world. Most of the projects undertake to study endangered ecosystems, biodiversity, and resource management, but a handful each year center on public health and sustainable development. For example, in 1998, volunteers worked with Ohio University's Dr. Prisca Nemapare in her study of maternal and child health in the Masvingo province of Zimbabwe, or helped former Peace Corps volunteer and nurse Phyllis Jansyn in her work to eliminate intestinal parasites in Cameroon. Each of these projects lasts two weeks. Project contributions range from $700 to $3000 and do not include airfare to the research site.

Explorations in Travel, Inc.

2458 River Road, Guilford, VT 05301
Tel: (802) 257-0152
Fax: (802) 257-2784
E-mail: explore@volunteertravel.com
Website: www.volunteertravel.com

Explorations in Travel provides individual volunteer work placements for students and adults from all over the world. Placements can be arranged in Belize, Costa Rica, Ecuador, Puerto Rico, and Guatemala. Work sites include schools, wildlife rehabilitation centers, animal shelters, and sustainable eco-tourism projects. Language classes can be incorporated into a placement. Fees are $975; there is a nonrefundable application fee of $35. Both individual and group programs are available. Explorations in Travel can also help with flight arrangements and fundraising ideas.

Fourth World Movement

7600 Willow Hill Drive, Landover, MD 20785-4658
Tel: (301) 336-9489
Fax: (301) 336-0092
E-mail: fourthworld@erols.com
Website: www.atd-fourthworld.org

Fourth World Movement's work is based on three priorities: learning from the most disadvantaged families, understanding how they become trapped in persistent poverty, and planning and developing projects with them. Summer work camps are available at the international center in France. Work camp volunteers are age eighteen and older and participate in a fourteen-day program in which they learn about poverty and do various kinds of manual labor.

(See listing under International Voluntary Service Organizations)

Global Citizens Network

130 North Howell Street, St. Paul, MN 55104
Tel: (800) 644-9292 or (651) 644-0960
E-mail: info@globalcitizens.org
Website: www.globalcitizens.org

Global Citizens Network (GCN) offers individuals the opportunity to interact with people of diverse cultures in order to develop creative and effective local solutions to global problems. GCN sends short-term teams of volunteers to communities in other countries. Each team is partnered with a grassroots organization active in meeting community needs. Volunteers assist and work under the direction of local people on locally initiated projects, staying with host families or living as a group at a community center. Each team member receives training materials and participates in an orientation session. Groups are led by GCN team leaders.

Tours last one to three weeks, including travel time. Program costs run from $600 to $1,650, airfare not included. Expenses are tax deductible in the United States. No specific skills are required. There are no upper age restrictions; underage volunteers must be accompanied by a parent or guardian. Current sites include Guatemala, Nepal, Kenya, Mexico, Peru, and Native American reservations in Arizona and New Mexico. Tasks range from school or road repair to water and sanitation projects to trail renovation.

Global Exchange

2017 Mission Street, Suite 303, San Francisco, CA 94110
Tel: (415) 255-7296
Fax: (415) 255-7498
E-mail: rt@globalexchange.org
Website: www.globalexchange.org

Global Exchange organizes reality tours, study seminars, and human rights delegations to more than twenty-five countries. These study tours offer a unique opportunity to learn firsthand about pressing issues confronting the developing world. Tour participants meet with peasant and labor organizers, community and religious leaders, peace activists, environmentalists, scholars, students, indigenous leaders, and government officials. Countries visited include South Africa, Zimbabwe, Cuba, Haiti, Israel/Palestine, Iran, Mexico (Chiapas and the US-Mexico border), Central America, Vietnam, Northern Ireland, Ecuador, Brazil, and Afghanistan. Costs range from $800 to $3,200. Global Exchange also offers Spanish language, dance, and bicycle trips to Cuba.

Heifer International

Attn: Study Tour Coordinator
425 West Capitol, Suite 800, Little Rock, AR 72202
Tel: (800) 422-0474
E-mail: studytours@heifer.org
Website: www.heifer.org

Heifer International is a worldwide community development organization that provides farm animals, as well as training and related agricultural and community-building services, to farmers in developing areas in forty-nine countries, and twenty-three states in the US. Heifer conducts eight- to ten-day study tours in countries where it has programs. Groups learn about development issues and may help build facilities. Volunteers pay their own expenses, which usually range from $1,000 to $3,000. For a list of currently offered study tours, go to the website.

(See listing under US Voluntary Service Organizations)

Ibike/Bicycle Africa

International Bicycle Fund
4887 Columbia Drive South, #Q, Seattle, WA 98108-1919
Tel/Fax (206) 767-0848
E-mail: ibike@ibike.org
Website: www.ibike.org

The International Bicycle Fund (IBF) arranges two- to four-week cultural immersion, educational bicycle tours in the US, Cuba, Ecuador, Vietnam, Nepal, Cameroon, Kenya, Uganda, Tanzania, Tunisia, Malawi, Eritrea, Ethiopia, Mali, Senegal, Gambia, Ghana, Togo, Benin, South Africa, Zimbabwe, and other African countries. Area specialists accompany each program. The cycling is moderate, and participants do not need to have extensive touring experience. Costs range from $900 to $2,500, not including airfare. The International Bicycle Fund promotes bicycle transportation, economic development, international understanding, and safety education.

Institute for Central American Development Studies

Dept. 826, PO Box 025216, Miami, FL 33102-5216
E-mail: icads@netbox.com
Website: www.icadscr.com
In Costa Rica:
Apartado 3 (2070), Sabanilla, San Jose, Costa Rica
Tel: 011 (506) 225-0508
Fax: 011 (506) 234-1337

The Institute for Central American Development Studies (ICADS) is a nonprofit center for research and analysis of Central American social and environmental issues. Four study and internship programs are offered. The first is a study-abroad/internship semester for undergrads combining four weeks of course work in Central American social justice topics and Spanish with a two-month internship with NGOs in Costa Rica or Nicaragua. Students return to ICADS in Costa Rica for written work and oral presentations at the end of their internship. The second is the fourteen-week Field Course in Resource Management and Sustainable Development, also for undergrads, which includes four weeks of intensive Spanish and urban studies, five weeks of group travel in the field, and five weeks of independent research. For undergrads, graduates, and professionals interested in Costa Rica, ICADS has a noncredit summer internship program comprising three weeks of Spanish study and seven weeks of intern service. ICADS also offers intensive Spanish language courses with a community service component or volunteer opportunity every month except December for students eighteen years and up.

The International Partnership for Service-Learning
815 Second Avenue, Suite 315, New York, NY 10017
Tel: (212) 986-0989
Fax: (212) 986-5039
E-mail: info@ipsl.org
Website: www.ipsl.org

The International Partnership for Service-Learning offers programs that integrate volunteer community service and formal academic study abroad for credit. Programs are available in the Czech Republic, Ecuador (Guayaquil and Quito), England, France, India, Israel, Jamaica, Mexico, the Philippines, Russia, Scotland, South Dakota (with Native Americans), South Africa, and Thailand. Each location offers a variety of community service projects, such as basic education, aid to the handicapped, women's issues, recreation, social welfare, and health. Costs range from $3,100 to $8,600 per term. Participants are primarily undergraduate students for summer, fall/spring, full-year or January and August intersessions. IPS-L also offers a one-year master's degree in International Service in Jamaica or Mexico (first semester) and the United Kingdom (second semester and thesis).

Interreligious Foundation for Community Organization/   R
Pastors for Peace
402 West 145th Street, New York, NY 10031
Tel: (212) 926-5757
Fax: (212) 926-5842
E-mail: ifco@igc.org
Website: www.ifconews.org

Pastors for Peace is an action and education project of the Interreligious Foundation for Community Organization (IFCO) and includes activists from all sectors of society. Pastors for Peace organizes humanitarian aid caravans, work brigades, delegations, and study tours to Mexico, Central America, and Cuba. Churches, schools, and other organizations can name the dates and help define the itinerary of customized study tours and construction brigades for their members. The cost ranges from $550 to $1,150, depending on the project. Call Pastors for Peace for more information and applications.

Los Niños

287 G Street, Chula Vista, CA 91910
Tel: (619) 426-9110
Fax: (619) 426-6664
E-mail: info@losninosinternational.org
Website: www.losninosinternational.org

Los Niños supports long-term community development projects in Tijuana, Mexicali, and San Diego. Programs include agriculture, organic gardening, and development education and are designed to promote self-reliance and social awareness. Los Niños offers weekend and week-long tour/seminar/work-project programs to US students who want to learn more about community development through hands-on participation. The cost varies according to length of stay. Los Niños is not religiously or politically affiliated in any way.

(See listing under International Voluntary Service Organizations)

Marazul Charters, Inc.

725 River Road, Edgewater, NJ 07020
Tel: (800) 223-5334 or (201) 840-6711
Fax: (201) 840-6719
E-mail: info@marazulcharters.com
Website: www.marazulcharters.com

Since 1979, Marazul has sent more than 300,000 people to Cuba. As a fully licensed Travel Service Provider, Marazul can assist licensed individuals and educational, cultural, and humanitarian groups with all aspects of travel, including air arrangements on direct flights from New York, Miami, and Los Angeles and flights through third countries such as Canada, Mexico, the Bahamas, and Jamaica; Cuban visas; and arrangements on the island from accommodations and transportation to meetings, visits, and exchanges. Special charters can be arranged for individual groups or organizations. Marazul is also a full-service travel agency and member of the American Society of Travel Agents, bilingual in Spanish and English, and ready to reserve your flights and hotels throughout the world.

Mexico Solidarity Network

4834 North Springfield, Chicago, IL 60625
Tel: (773) 583-7728
E-mail: msn@mexicosolidarity.org
Website: www.mexicosolidarity.org

Mexico Solidarity Network (MSN) is a network of US grassroots organizations supporting economic and social justice and democracy on both sides of the US-Mexico border, with special attention to globalization and the indigenous population of Chiapas. MSN sponsors speaking tours for Mexican activists to the US and educational delegations to Mexico.

Middle East Children's Alliance

905 Parker Street, Berkeley, CA 94710
Tel: (510) 548-0542
Fax: (510) 548-0543
E-mail: meca@mecaforpeace.org
Website: www.mecaforpeace.org

The Middle East Children's Alliance raises funds for humanitarian aid (medical supplies, schoolbooks, food, and clothing) for children in Iraq and the West Bank in Gaza. They sponsor short-term delegations several times a year to Palestine and Israel. These delegates meet with Israeli peace activists and visit Palestinian NGOs, production cooperatives, refugee camps, health clinics, and kindergartens in the West Bank and Gaza. Costs of programs vary.

(See listing under International Voluntary Service Organizations)

Minnesota Studies in International Development

University of Minnesota, Global Campus Study Abroad
230 Heller Hall, 271 19th Avenue South, Minneapolis, MN 55455
Tel: (612) 626-9000
Fax: (612) 626-8009
E-mail: UMabroad@umn.edu
Website: www.UMabroad.umn.edu

Minnesota Studies in International Development (MSID) combines intensive classroom work with individualized field placements and research opportunities in grassroots development and social change projects in rural and urban settings alike. MSID offers programs in Ecuador, Ghana, India, Kenya, and Senegal, with two enrollment options at each site—academic year and fall semester only.

Participants study international development theory, cross-cultural communication, history and culture, and local language during the first portion of the fall semester. The classroom period is followed by a field placement which serves as a laboratory for the concepts and theories discussed in the classroom. Typical categories for field placements and internships include public health, education, environmental protection, social services, and agriculture.

Mobility International USA

PO Box 10767, Eugene, OR 97440 or 45 West Broadway, Suite 202, Eugene, OR 97401
Tel: (541) 343-1284 (voice/TTY)
Fax: (541) 343-6812
E-mail: info@miusa.org
Website: www.miusa.org

Mobility International USA's (MIUSA) international exchanges specialize in leadership training, community service, cross-cultural experiential learning, and advocacy for the rights and inclusion of people with disabilities. These short-term group exchanges for youth, adults, and professionals with and without disabilities take place in the United States and abroad. MIUSA has coordinated exchanges with Azerbaijan, Bulgaria, China, Costa Rica, East Asia, Germany, Italy, Japan, Mexico, Russia, the United Kingdom, and other countries. Activities include training seminars and workshops, adaptive recreational activities, cross-cultural communication, language classes, and volunteer service projects. Exchanges vary from ten days to three weeks in length.

MIUSA's National Clearinghouse on Disability and Exchange (NCDE) provides additional information on international exchange and volunteer and community service opportunities. NCDE staff can respond to inquiries on the range of opportunities available and on how people with disabilities can make these possibilities a reality.

Nicaragua Network

1247 E Street SE, Washington, DC 20003
Tel: (202) 544-9355
Fax: (202) 544-9359
E-mail: nicanet@afgj.org
Website:www.nicanet.org

The Nicaragua Network advocates for sound US foreign policies toward Nicaragua and provides information and organizing tools to a network of 200 solidarity and peace and justice committees across the United States. The network organizes speaking tours of Nicaraguans in the US and study tours to Nicaragua.

(See listing under International Voluntary Service Organizations)

Our Developing World

13004 Paseo Presada, Saratoga, CA 95070-4125
Tel: (408) 379-4431
Fax: (408) 376-0755
E-mail: odw@magiclink.net
Website: www.magiclink.net/~odw

The main focus of Our Developing World (ODW) is to bring the realities of the developing world and the richness of diverse cultures to North Americans through programs in schools, churches, and community groups. Once a year, ODW leads "non-Hilton reality tours of hope." They take small groups of travelers to see for themselves and hear the stories of the voiceless. Past destinations have included Cuba, Nicaragua, Honduras, Guatemala, Mozambique, Zimbabwe, South Africa, the Philippines, Vietnam, Cambodia, Laos, and Indigenous Hawaii. The tours provide an opportunity to talk with peasants, workers, women's associations, health workers, and co-op members, as well as a chance to learn about health, agrarian reform, human rights and educational campaigns, and economic and social planning.

Plowshares Institute

PO Box 243, Simsbury, CT 06070
Tel: (860) 651-4304
Fax: (860) 651-4305
E-mail: PlowsharesCT@cs.com
Website: www.plowsharesinstitute.org

Plowshares tours initiate cross-cultural dialogue between peoples of developed and developing nations. Participants commit to both advance preparation and community education work upon their return. Trip itineraries include meetings with religious and civic leaders, homestay experiences, and visits to development projects. The institute plans two-week programs to several countries, including South Africa, China, Indonesia, Cuba, Brazil, Uganda, and South America. Please refer to the Plowshares Institute website.

El Porvenir

2508 42nd Street, Sacramento, CA 95817
Tel: (916) 736-3663
Fax: (916) 227-5068
E-mail: info@elporvenir.org
Website: www.elporvenir.org

El Porvenir supports sustainable infrastructure development in poor rural communities in Nicaragua through funding and technical aid to locally originated potable water, sanitation, and reforestation projects. El Porvenir sponsors one-week and two-week work trips and one-week educational tours to Nicaragua six times each year. The cost of the educational tour is $950 per person, plus airfare to Nicaragua; the cost of the work tour is $900 for two weeks and $750 for one week, plus airfare. Work tour participants stay in simple hostels and assist with a construction project. Educational tours visit various El Porvenir project villages and engage in cultural and recreational activities. No Spanish is required, and no construction experience is required for the work tour. Work groups are limited to ten people. All groups are accompanied at all times by bilingual El Porvenir staff.

School for International Training

Global Partnership Program
Kipling Road, PO Box 676, Brattleboro, VT 05302-0676
Tel: (802) 257-7751 or (800) 257-7751
Fax: (802) 258-3248
E-mail: egp@sit.edu
Website: www.sit.edu/gp or www.global-partnership.net

The Global Partnership (GP) offers uniquely relevant, international-quality, professional education opportunities for the leaders, managers, and staff of nongovernmental organizations (NGOs) and other civil society organizations around the world. Online and face-to-face courses of the NGO Leadership and Management curriculum are based on learning experiences with Global Partnership faculty and participants. The program offers three options toward a degree. Participants can earn the Postgraduate Diploma in NGO Leadership and Management through BRAC (Bangladesh), involving three months of full-time classroom studies in Bangladesh and Nepal, a practicum in the participant's own organization or anywhere else in the world, and a final seminar in Bangladesh, or through Escuela para el Dasarrollo (Peru) or IIRR (the Philippines), involving short residence, online courses or part-time studies over a period of one or more years, a practicum, and a final seminar. Participants who earn the postgraduate diploma are eligible to apply to an accelerated program leading to the Master of International and Intercultural Management degree through SIT. The remaining eighteen credits are completed in one semester at SIT's Brattleboro, Vermont, campus between February and May each year. Coursework includes policy advocacy, financial resource management, interorganizational relations, NGO management systems, and NGO capacity building.

The Sokoni Safari

Bridges to Community
PO Box 35, Scarborough, New York, NY 10510
Tel: (914) 923-2200
International Communities for the Renewal of the Earth
PO Box 194, Cross River, NY 10518
Tel: (914) 763-5790
E-mail: sarahg@igc.org

The Sokoni Safari, a joint project of Bridges to Community and International Communities for the Renewal of the Earth, is a two-week trip to Kenya organized and managed largely by the staff of the Greenbelt Movement, one of East Africa's foremost environmental organizations. Participants will stay with Greenbelt at their Nairobi headquarters, learning about its work and about Kenyan culture and politics. They will also travel to rural Kenya, staying with families in a village and assisting with agricultural tasks. Throughout the tour, participants examine cultural differences along with the problematic relations between the global North and the global South in a postcolonial context with respect to international lending institutions, consumer markets, and lifestyles. The cost of the fourteen-day journey is $2,000 per person plus airfare, $1,500 per person plus airfare for students. Limited partial scholarships are available. The fee includes accommodations, meals, internal travel, and a contribution to the Greenbelt Movement. Contact either of the above phone numbers for further information and reservations.

Third World Opportunities Program

779 Fulton Road, San Marcos, CA 92069
Tel: (760) 471-7652
E-mail: severinelaine@aol.com

The Third World Opportunities Program (TWO) is a hunger and poverty awareness program designed to provide opportunities for appropriate responses to human need. It seeks to encourage sensitivity to life in the developing world; intentional reflection on our relationship with people in the developing world; effective work projects that offer practical services to the hungry, homeless, and the poor; and organized efforts to change existing conditions. TWO offers a two-pronged program consisting of an awareness tour along the US-Mexico border followed by a short-term work project such as a six-day service assignment at orphanages in Tecate and Las Palmas, Mexico. The cost is $225 for the six-day journey from San Diego, which includes meals, accommodations, administration, building materials, and support of the orphanages.

Ufufuo, Inc.   R

1225 Geranium Street NW, Washington, DC 20012
Tel: (202) 722-1461
Fax: (202) 723-5376
E-mail: hjconfer@worldnet.att.net
Contact: Harold Confer, director

Ufufuo, Inc., is a public charity that responds to human-caused disasters with interfaith and, when possible, international volunteers interested in helping rebuild mosques or synagogues burned as a result of patriotic hate crimes. Projects are planned as congregations find the resources to help them rebuild and request Ufufuo's assistance. Contact the director, Harold Confer, at the e-mail above to get the latest news and location of projects. Volunteers must commit to a minimum of one week, or three weeks for international volunteers. The cost is $150 to $165 per week for room, board, housing, and job oversight. Volunteers are required to have health insurance and provide their own transportation to and from the project.

US Servas

11 John Street, #505, New York, NY 10038
Tel: (212) 267-0252
E-mail: info@usservas.org
Website: www.usservas.org

US Servas fosters a more just and peaceful world by promoting appreciation of cultural differences through homestays and experiences in hosts' communities. Travelers are invited to share life in the home and community and their concerns about social and international problems for short two-night stays. Some hosts offer longer visits. Membership application for travelers consists of an interview, two character references, and a $65 membership fee per adult. Prospective hosts must also be interviewed and fill out an application. To receive an application, send a SASE or visit the website to download one.

Venceremos Brigade

PO Box 30906, Oakland, CA 94612
Tel: (415) 267-0606
E-mail: vbsfbay@yahoo.com
Website: www.vbrigade.org

Venceremos Brigade participants travel for two weeks to Cuba; visit schools, factories, clinics, and hospitals; have informal visits and discussions with Cubans; and participate in educational seminars with representatives from other countries. Brigade members participate in work camp activities. Each participant must be at least eighteen years old, be a US citizen and have a valid passport, and not be currently in the military service. Upon acceptance, participants attend a required series of preparatory sessions and commit to work in some aspect of Brigade education projects upon return. They are expected to pay transportation and miscellaneous expenses. Brigade committees are located in various areas throughout the US.

Voices on the Border Educational Delegations

1600 Webster Street NE, Washington, DC 20017
Tel: (202) 529-2912
Fax: (202) 529-0897
E-mail: voices@votb.org
Website: www.votb.org

Voices on the Border promotes community partnerships between rural communities of repatriated refugees in eastern El Salvador and

interested individuals and groups in the US. Delegations to visit partner communities are facilitated by Voices several times a year and
generally last for ten to twelve days. These trips are usually organized
by existing partner groups, but other individuals are often welcome to
join them on one of these travel experiences. The cost of participating is approximately $75 per day, per person, for in-country basic
needs, including housing, food, transportation, and translator.
Airfare, visas, and other incidental costs are not included.

World-Wide Opportunities on Organic Farms Independents
PO Box 2675, Lewes, East Sussex, BN7 1RB, United Kingdom
Tel/Fax: 011 (44 0) 1273-476-286
E-mail: hello@wwoof.org
Website: www.wwoof.org

World-Wide Opportunities on Organic Farms (WWOOF)
Independents provides those who would like to volunteer on organic
farms with a list of host farms throughout the world. The purpose of
WWOOF is to enable people to learn firsthand about organic growing techniques, expose urban dwellers to farm life and work, and help
farmers make organic production a viable alternative. WWOOF
organizations exist in many countries, and WWOOF host farms exist
even in countries without a WWOOF headquarters. Among the
nations represented are Brazil, Cambodia, Chile, Costa Rica,
Ecuador, Ghana, India, Ivory Coast, Malaysia, Sri Lanka, and Togo,
as well as several European countries, Australia, and New Zealand. If
you would like to volunteer in a given country, contact the country's
WWOOF organization; if there isn't one, contact WWOOF
Independents in the United Kingdom, either through its website or
by writing to the above address and enclosing a SASE and an international reply coupon, available at any post office. A list of national
WWOOF organizations can be found on the website.

Farm opportunities vary in the amount of skill or experience
expected, but many hosts require none. Room and board are provided
at all sites. Volunteers should keep in mind that WWOOF is merely
a contact service. It provides the address of the farm, but the volunteer must work out the placement with the host and obtain any necessary visas and work permits.

Resources

Other Organizations

These groups do not generally sponsor intern or travel programs; they distribute information about volunteer or travel opportunities, foreign countries, underrepresented cultures, or aspects of development.

Bank Information Center

733 15th Street NW, Suite 1126, Washington, DC 20005
Tel: (202) 737-7752
Fax: (202) 737-1155
E-mail: info@bicusa.org
Website: www.bicusa.org

Bank Information Center (BIC) provides hard-to-obtain information on the projects and policies of multilateral development banks (like the World Bank) to environmental and social justice organizations in developing countries. BIC offers numerous publications and reports and advocates for greater transparency in World Bank operations. There is much documentation here of the processes by which development is managed and mismanaged.

The Center for Community Change

1000 Wisconsin Avenue NW, Washington, DC 20007
Tel: (202) 342-0567
Fax: (202) 333-5462

West Coast Office:
3655 South Grand Avenue, #250, Los Angeles, CA 90007
Tel: (213) 743-3940

E-mail: info@communitychange.org
Website: www.communitychange.org

For more than thirty years, the Center for Community Change (CCC) has helped grassroots organizations build their communities' capacity for self-help by training community organizers and providing technical assistance to community organizations. The website contains information on aspects of poverty in the US—including housing, jobs, transportation, health, and policy—and profiles of advocacy projects with which CCC has assisted. The site also includes downloadable reports, the online newsletter *Organizing* (focusing on the welfare reform debate), policy alerts, facts and figures on wealth distribution, a list of groups besides CCC that train community organizers, and brochures aimed at grassroots groups with titles such as *How to Lobby without Regrets* and *Get Me to the Polls On Time.*

CIVICUS: World Alliance for Citizen Participation

919 18th Street NW, 3rd Floor, Washington, DC 20006
Tel: (202) 331-8518
Fax: (202) 331-8774
E-mail: info@civicus.org
Website: www.civicus.org

CIVICUS is an international alliance dedicated to strengthening citizen action and civil society throughout the world, especially in areas where participatory democracy and freedom of citizen association are threatened. The website contains links to its multitude of membership NGOs. The organization publishes books and a bimonthly newsletter following trends and offering analyses on the third sector movement worldwide. Its atlas, available free online as well as in other formats, profiles the state of civil society in dozens of countries—size and scope, economic impact, legal and tax framework, state of relations with government and business sectors, and names of resource organizations.

Civil Society International

2929 NE Blakeley Street, Seattle, WA 98105
Tel: (206) 523-4755
E-mail: csi@civilsoc.org
Website: www.civilsoc.org

Civil Society International (CSI) assists independent organizations worldwide working for freedom and civil society in nations unfriendly to these principles. It provides assistance mainly in the form of information, networking, and educational resources.

Council on International Educational Exchange

7 Custom House Street, 3rd Floor, Portland, ME 04101
Tel: (800) 407-8839
Fax: (207) 553-7699
E-mail: studyinfo@ciee.org
Website: www.ciee.org

Council on International Educational Exchange (CIEE) offers a range of study abroad, travel, volunteer, and internship programs for youth, college students, recent graduates, and teachers.

Cultural Survival, Inc.

221 Prospect Street, Cambridge, MA 02139
Tel: (617) 441-5400
Fax: (617) 441-5417
E-mail: csinc@cs.org
Website: www.cs.org

Cultural Survival, Inc., promotes the cause of self-determination for indigenous peoples worldwide, provides organizational support and fiscal sponsorship for projects in indigenous communities, and publishes reports on a host of topics relating to development.

Focus on the Global South

c/o CUSRI, Chulalongkorn University
Bangkok 10330 Thailand
Tel: 011 (66 2) 218-7363 or 011 (66 2) 218-7364 or 011 (66 2) 218-7365
Fax: 011 (66 2) 255-9976
E-mail: admin@focusweb.org
Website: www.focusweb.org

Focus on the Global South supports a program of progressive development policy research and practice dedicated to regional and global policy analysis and advocacy work. Its emphasis is on the developing nations of the Southern Hemisphere, particularly the Asia-Pacific region. Many of Focus' articles and reports are available online. Focus has accepted several short-term interns and volunteers in the past. Priorities are on applicants from the South, who are self-funding and have skills that match Focus campaign and program needs at the particular time. Due to limited office and staff capacity, usually only one person is accepted at a time.

Fund for Reconciliation and Development

355 West 39th Street, New York, NY 10018
Tel: (212) 760-9903
Fax: (212) 760-9906
E-mail: info@ffrd.org
Website: www.ffrd.org

Fund for Reconciliation and Development (FRD) promotes cooperation between US nonprofit organizations and their counterparts in Vietnam, Laos, Cambodia, and Cuba. FRD organizes conferences in the United States and publishes a quarterly newsletter, *Interchange*.

Grassroots International

179 Boylston Street, 4th Floor, Boston, MA 02130
Tel: (617) 524-1400
Fax: (617) 524-5525
Website: www.grassrootsonline.org

Through cash grants and material aid, Grassroots International supports the work of NGOs in Haiti, Mexico, Brazil, Eritrea, Palestine, and East Timor. It also performs education and advocacy on a range of issues.

InterAction: American Council for Voluntary International Action

1717 Massachusetts Avenue NW, Suite 701,
Washington, DC 20036
Tel: (202) 667-8227
Fax: (202) 667-8236
E-mail: publications@interaction.org
Website: www.interaction.org

InterAction is the largest alliance of US-based international development and humanitarian nongovernmental organizations. With more than 160 members operating in every developing country, InterAction works to overcome poverty, exclusion, and suffering by advancing social justice and basic dignity for all. InterAction publishes *Monday Developments*, a biweekly newsletter that provides in-depth news and commentary on global trends that affect relief, refugee, and development work, as well as listing job opportunities throughout the world. InterAction also publishes *Member Profiles*, a biannual directory of its members; *Global Work*, a guide for volunteer, internship, and fellowship opportunities in international development abroad; and a weekly e-mail listing of extensive employment and internship opportunities in the international development and assistance field. For subscriptions, job listings, or advertising, please contact Nicole Duciaume at (202) 667-8227, ext. 121, or at nduciaume@interaction.org.

International Development Exchange

827 Valencia Street, Suite 101, San Francisco, CA 94110
Tel: (415) 824-8384
E-mail: info@idex.org
Website: www.idex.org

International Development Exchange (IDEX) forms partnerships with grassroots economic empowerment organizations in Africa, Asia, and Latin America. We support our partners through grant making, information sharing, and alliance-building activities, while actively educating people in the US about our partners' work.

The International Ecotourism Society

733 15th Street NW, Suite 1000,
Washington, DC 20005
Tel: (202) 347-9203
Fax: (202) 387-7915
E-mail: ecomail@ecotourism.org
Website: www.ecotourism.org

The International Ecotourism Society (TIES) is an international membership organization dedicated to disseminating information about ecologically sound and sustainable tourism. Individual memberships start at $35 per year and include subscription to a newsletter, discounts on TIES publications, and access to lists of tour and lodge operators.

International Volunteer Programs Association

c/o AFS International, 71 West 23rd Street, 17th Floor,
New York, NY 10010
Tel: (212) 807-8686, ext. 150
Fax: (212) 807-1001
E-mail: international_IVPA@yahoo.com
Website: www.volunteerinternational.org

The International Volunteer Programs Association (IVPA) is an alliance
of nonprofit nongovernmental organizations based in the Americas that
are involved in international volunteer and internship exchanges. IVPA's
website has a database of volunteer opportunities as well as general
advice on fundraising and traveling abroad.

Transitions Abroad Publishing

18 Hulst Road, PO Box 1300, Amherst, MA 01002
Tel: (413) 256-3414
Fax: (413) 256-0373
E-mail: info@transitionsabroad.com
Website: www.transitionsabroad.com

For twenty-six years, Transitions Abroad has published comprehensive
guides, directories, and books with practical information on alternatives
to mass tourism: living, working, studying abroad, and vacationing with
the people of the host country. The emphasis is on enriching, informed,
affordable, and responsible travel. Visit the website or contact
Transitions Abroad for more information or copies of their publications.

Volunteers for Peace International Voluntary Service

1034 Tiffany Road, Belmont, VT 05730
Tel: (802) 259-2759
Fax: (802) 259-2922
E-mail: vfp@vfp.org
Website: www.vfp.org

Volunteers for Peace Publishes *The International Workcamp Directory*
($20 first-class postage paid), an annual booklet listing over 2,200
opportunities for meaningful travel throughout Western and Eastern
Europe, Russia, Africa, Asia, Australia, and Latin America. Work camps
are affordable ways that North Americans of all ages can promote international goodwill through short-term community service projects in
eighty countries. Two- to three-week programs cost $200 including
room and board. Please call, write, or e-mail for the 2003 directory.

WorkingAbroad

2nd Floor Office Suite, 59, Lansdowne Place, Hove, East Sussex, BN3 1FL England
Tel/Fax: 011 (44 0) 1273-711-406
E-mail: info@workingabroad.com
Website: www.workingabroad.com

WorkingAbroad runs a database of organizations looking for volunteers in the humanitarian and environmental domains. People interested can receive personalized reports according to their skills and interests. These reports cost $45 if sent by e-mail and $56 for a hard copy. More information on this service can be found at their website.

Guides to International Voluntary Service

How to Live Your Dream of Volunteering Overseas. Joseph Collins, Stefano DeZerega, and Zahara Heckscher (New York: Penguin Books, 2002). Penguin USA, 375 Hudson Street, New York, NY 10014-3658, Tel: (212) 366-2000, Fax: (212) 366-2469.

The International Directory of Voluntary Work, eighth edition. Victoria Pybus (Oxford: Vacation Work Publications, 2002). Distributed in the US by The Globe Pequot Press, 246 Goose Lane, PO Box 480, Guilford, CT 06437, Tel: (800) 243-0495, Fax: (800) 820-2329, Website: *www.globepequot.com.*

International Directory of Youth Internships: With the United Nations, Its Specialized Agencies, and Non-Governmental Organizations. Michael Culligan and Cynthia T. Morehouse, eds. (New York: Apex Press, 1994). The Apex Press, PO Box 337, Croton-on-Hudson, NY 10520, Tel: (800) 316-APEX or (914) 271-6500, Website: *www.cipa-apex.org.*

The Peace Corps and More: 175 Ways to Work, Study and Travel in the Third World. Medea Benjamin and Miya Rodolfo-Sioson. (San Francisco: Global Exchange, 2003). Global Exchange, 2017 Mission Street, Suite 303, San Francisco, CA 94110, Tel: (800) 505-4410, Website: *http://store.globalexchange.org.*

Social Change through Voluntary Action. M. L. Dantwala, et al. (Thousand Oaks, CA: Sage Publications, Inc., 1998). Sage Publications, Inc., 2455

Teller Road, Thousand Oaks, CA 91320, Tel: (805) 499-0721, Website: *www.sagepub.com.*

Working for Global Justice Directory (San Francisco: JustAct, 1999), JustAct, 333 Valencia Street, Suite 325, San Francisco, CA 94103, Tel: (415) 431-4204.

Guides to US Voluntary Service

Internships 2004 (Lawrenceville, NJ: Peterson's Guides, 2004). Peterson's Guides, PO Box 67005, Lawrenceville, NJ 08648, Tel: (800) 338-3282, Website: *www.petersons.com.*

A World of Options: A Guide to International Educational Exchange and Travel for Persons with Disabilities. Christa Bucks. (Eugene, OR: Mobility International, 1997). Mobility International USA, PO Box 10767, Eugene, OR 97440, Tel: (541) 343-1284.

Publications on Travel and Tourism

Whether you intend to travel or volunteer abroad, the higher-quality tourist guides can provide background on the history, political situation, customs, and culture of countries or regions that interest you. Check the travel section of your local bookstore or contact the publishers of the series below.

Travel Publishers
Lonely Planet Publications, Lonely Planet USA
150 Linden Street, Oakland CA 94607
Tel: (510) 893-8555
Fax: (510) 893-8563
E-mail: info@lonelyplanet.com
Website: www.lonelyplanet.com
Lonely Planet has an especially rich and detailed website, featuring bulletin boards, e-mail discussions, and up-to-the-minute information on numerous countries.

Moon Travel Handbooks
(covering the Americas, Asia, and the Pacific)

Avalon Travel Publishing
1400 65th Street, Suite 250, Emeryville, CA 94608
Tel: (510) 595-3664
Fax: (510) 595-4228
Website: www.moon.com

Rough Guides USA
345 Hudson Street, 4th Floor, New York, NY 10014
Tel: (212) 414-3635
Website: www.roughguides.com

Travel Guides

Alternative Travel Directory: The Complete Guide to Work, Study and Travel Overseas, seventh edition. Clayton Hubbs and David Cline, eds. (Amherst, MA: Transitions Abroad Publishing, Inc., 2002). Transitions Abroad Publishing, 18 Hulst Road, PO Box 1300, Amherst, MA 01002, Tel: (413) 256-3414, Website: *www.transitionsabroad.com.*

Fodor's Great American Learning Vacations, 1997, second edition. (New York: Fodor's Travel Publications, 1997). Random House, 1540 Broadway, New York, NY 10036.

Free Vacations and Bargain Adventures in the USA. Evelyn Kaye. (Boulder, CO: Blue Panda Publications, 1998). Blue Panda Publications, 3031 Fifth Street, Boulder, CO 80304.

Rethinking Tourism, second edition. Deborah McLaren. (Bloomfield, CT: Kumarian Press, 2003). Kumarian Press, 1294 Blue Hills Avenue, Bloomfield, CT 06002, Tel: (800) 289-2664 or (860) 243-2098.

Transitions Abroad. Transitions Abroad Publishing, Inc., 18 Hulst Road, PO Box 1300, Amherst, MA 01002, Tel: (413) 256-3414, Website: *www.transitionsabroad.com.* A bimonthly publication.

Volunteer Vacations: Short-Term Adventures That Will Benefit You and Others, eighth edition. Bill McMillon et al., eds. (Chicago, IL: Chicago Review Press, 2003). Chicago Review Press, 814 North Franklin, Chicago, IL 60610.

Resources for Finding Jobs in Development

Careers in International Affairs, seventh edition. School of Foreign Service (Washington, DC: Georgetown University Press, 2003). Georgetown University Press, 3240 Prospect Street, NW, Washington, DC 20007, Tel: (202) 687-5889, Website: *www.press.georgetown.edu.*

International Career Employment Weekly and *International Employment Hotline* (monthly). International Career Employment Center, Carlyle Corporation, 1088 Middle River Road, Stanardsville, VA 22973, Tel: (434) 985-6444, Fax: (434) 985-6828, E-mail: Lisa@internationaljobs.org, Website: *www.internationaljobs.org.* Both publications contain extensive overseas job listings in the public and private sectors. Orientation is toward skilled professionals. The center also publishes an annual guide to overseas internships.

Work Abroad 2002, fourth edition. (Amherst, MA: Transitions Abroad Publishing, Inc., 2002). Transitions Abroad Publishing, 18 Hulst Road, PO Box 1300, Amherst, MA 01002, Tel: (413) 256-3414, Website: *www.transitionsabroad.com.*

Working for Global Justice Directory. (San Francisco: JustAct, 1999). JustAct, 333 Valencia Street, Suite 325, San Francisco, CA 94103, Tel: (415) 431-4204.

Online Resources

Association of Voluntary Service Organizations
Website: *www.avso.org*

Association of national and international nonprofits based in Europe. Site contains volunteer opportunities, links, and a bulletin board.

Grass-roots.org
Website: *www.grass-roots.org*

Lively descriptions of over 200 grassroots organizations in the United States working in diverse and often innovative ways to eliminate poverty. Robin Garr, creator of the website, has also authored a book, *Reinvesting in America*, with many more program descriptions, along with a "Getting Involved" appendix list of groups that need volunteers.

Idealist (a project of Action without Borders)
Website: *www.idealist.org*

Lists thousands of volunteer opportunities and nonprofit jobs; offers publications and resources for nonprofits and consultants.

Project Cooperating for Cooperation
Website: *www.coop4coop.org*

Comprehensive directory of development organizations and volunteer programs.

Further Reading

Broder, David S. "AmeriCorps Suddenly Hit With 'Devastating' Cutbacks," *San Francisco Chronicle*, June 14, 2003, p. A4.

Chasin, Barbara H. and Richard W. Franke. *Kerala: Radical Reform as Development in an Indian State*. Oakland, CA: Food First Books, 1994.

Chinn, Erica and Kristina Taylor, eds. *The Pros and Cons of the Peace Corps*. San Francisco: JustAct.

CIVICUS. *Civil Society at the Millennium*. West Hartford, CT: Kumarian Press, 1999.

Collins, Joseph, Stefano DeZerega, and Zahara Heckscher. *How to Live Your Dream of Volunteering Overseas*. New York: Penguin Books, 2002.

Collins, Joseph, Frances Moore Lappé, and Peter Rosset with Luis Esparza. *World Hunger: Twelve Myths*. New York: Grove Press, 1998.

Etzioni, Amitai. "How Not to Squander the Volunteer Spirit," *The Christian Science Monitor*, January 27, 2003, p. 11.

Fischer, Fritz. *Making Them Like Us: Peace Corps Volunteers in the 1960s.* Washington, DC: Smithsonian Institution Press, 1998.

Kutzner, Patricia L. and Nicola Lagoudakis, with Teresa Eyring. *Who's Involved with Hunger: An Organization Guide for Education and Advocacy.* Washington, DC: World Hunger Education Service, 1995.

Lappé, Frances Moore and Rachel Schurman. *Taking Population Seriously*. Oakland, CA: Food First Books, 1990.

MacMartin, Charley. "Peace Corps and Empire," *Covert Action Quarterly*, Winter 1991–1992, no. 39.

"One Pledge Fits All," *The San Francisco Chronicle*, November 29, 2002, p. A28.

Razzi, Elizabeth. "What the Peace Corps Can Do For You," *Kiplinger's Personal Finance Magazine*, June 1998.

Reeves, T. Zane. *The Politics of the Peace Corps and VISTA*. Tuscaloosa, AL: University of Alabama Press, 1988.

"Russia, Citing Changing Needs, Ends Its Tie with Peace Corps," *The New York Times*, December 28, 2002, p. A4.

Schwarz, Karen. *What You Can Do for Your Country: Inside the Peace Corps—A Thirty-Year History*. New York: William Morrow, 1993.

Shahinian, Mark. "Healing Africa: Peace Corps Plan Not Enough," *Milwaukee Journal Sentinel*, September 3, 2002, p. 13A.

Zimmerman, Jonathan. "Beyond Double Consciousness: Black Peace Corps Volunteers in Africa, 1961–1971," *Journal of American History*, December 1995, vol. 82, no. 3.

Alphabetical Index

Geographical Index

Africa

Asia

South America, Central America, Caribbean

MORE BOOKS FROM FOOD FIRST

Sustainable Agriculture and Development: Transforming Food Production in Cuba

Fernando Funes, Luis García, Martin Bourque, Nilda Pérez, and Peter Rosset

Unable to import food or farm chemicals and machines in the wake of the Soviet bloc's collapse and a tightening US embargo, Cuba turned toward sustainable agriculture, organic farming, urban gardens, and other techniques to secure its food supply. This book gives details of that remarkable achievement.

Paperback, $18.95

The Future in the Balance: Essays on Globalization and Resistance

Walden Bello

Edited with a preface by Anuradha Mittal

A new collection of essays by Third World activist and scholar Walden Bello on the myths of development as prescribed by the World Trade Organization and other institutions, and the possibility of another world based on fairness and justice.

Paperback, $13.95

Views from the South: The Effects of Globalization and the WTO on Third World Countries

Foreword by Jerry Mander

Afterword by Anuradha Mittal

Edited by Sarah Anderson

This rare collection of essays by Third World activists and scholars describes in pointed detail the effects of the WTO and other Bretton Woods institutions.

Paperback, $12.95

Basta! Land and the Zapatista Rebellion in Chiapas

Revised edition

George A. Collier with Elizabeth Lowery Quaratiello

Foreword by Peter Rosset

The classic on the Zapatistas in a new revised edition, including a preface by Roldolfo Stavenhagen, a new epilogue about the present challenges to the indigenous movement in Chiapas, and an updated bibliography.

Paperback, $14.95

America Needs Human Rights

Edited by Anuradha Mittal and Peter Rosset

This new anthology includes writings on understanding human rights, poverty in America, and welfare reform and human rights.

Paperback, $13.95

The Paradox of Plenty: Hunger in a Bountiful World

Excerpts from Food First's best writings on world hunger and what we can do to change it.

Paperback, $18.95

Education for Action: Graduate Studies with a Focus on Social Change

Fourth edition

Edited by Joan Powell

A newly updated authoritative and easy-to-use guidebook that provides information on progressive programs in a wide variety of fields.

Paperback, $12.95

We encourage you to buy Food First books from your local independent bookseller: if they don't have them in stock, they can usually order them for you fast. To find an independent bookseller in your area, go to *www.booksense.com*.

Food First books are also available through the major online booksellers (Powell's, Amazon, and Barnes and Noble), and through the Food First website, *www.foodfirst.org*. You can also order direct from our distributor, CDS, at (800) 343-4499. If you have trouble locating a Food First title, write, call, or e-mail us:

Food First
398 60th Street
Oakland, CA 94618, USA
PHONE (510) 654-4400
FAX (510) 654-4551
E-MAIL foodfirst@foodfirst.org
WEB www.foodfirst.org

If you are a bookseller or other reseller, contact our distributor, CDS, at (800) 343-4499, to order.

ABOUT FOOD FIRST

Food First, also known as the Institute for Food and Development Policy, is a nonprofit research and education-for-action center dedicated to investigating and exposing the root causes of hunger in a world of plenty. It was founded in 1975 by Frances Moore Lappé, author of the bestseller *Diet for a Small Planet,* and food policy analyst Dr. Joseph Collins. Food First research has revealed that hunger is created by concentrated economic and political power, not by scarcity. Resources and decision-making are in the hands of a wealthy few, depriving the majority of land, jobs, and therefore food.

Hailed by the *New York Times* as "one of the most established food think tanks in the country," Food First has grown to profoundly shape the debate about hunger and development.

But Food First is more than a think tank. Through books, reports, videos, media appearances, and speaking engagements, Food First experts not only reveal the often hidden roots of hunger, they show how individuals can get involved in bringing an end to the problem. Food First inspires action by bringing to light the courageous efforts of people around the world who are creating farming and food systems that truly meet people's needs.

HOW TO BECOME A MEMBER OR INTERN OF FOOD FIRST

BECOME A MEMBER OF FOOD FIRST

Private contributions and membership gifts form the financial base of Food First/Institute for Food and Development Policy. The success of the Institute's programs depends not only on its dedicated volunteers and staff, but on financial activists as well. Each member strengthens Food First's efforts to change a hungry world. We invite you to join Food First. As a member you will receive a 20 percent discount on all Food First books. You will also receive our quarterly publication, *Food First News and Views,* and timely *Backgrounders* that provide information and suggestions for action on current food and hunger crises in the United States and around the world. If you want to subscribe to our Internet newsletters, *Food Rights Watch* and *We Are Fighting Back,* send us an e-mail at foodfirst@foodfirst.org. All contributions are tax-deductible.

BECOME AN INTERN FOR FOOD FIRST

There are opportunities for interns in research, advocacy, campaigning, publishing, computers, media, and publicity at Food First. Our interns come from around the world. They are a vital part of our organization and make our work possible.

To become a member or apply to become an intern, just call, visit our website, or clip and return the attached coupon to

Food First/Institute for Food and Development Policy
398 60th Street, Oakland, CA 94618, USA
PHONE (510) 654-4400
FAX (510) 654-4551
E-MAIL foodfirst@foodfirst.org
WEB www.foodfirst.org

You are also invited to give a gift membership to others interested in the fight to end hunger.

JOINING FOOD FIRST

☐ I want to join Food First and receive a 20% discount on this and all subsequent orders. Enclosed is my tax-deductible contribution of:

☐ $35   ☐ $50   ☐ $100   ☐ $1,000   ☐ OTHER

NAME _____

ADDRESS _____

CITY/STATE/ZIP _____

DAYTIME PHONE (_____) _____

E-MAIL _____

ORDERING FOOD FIRST MATERIALS

ITEM DESCRIPTION	QTY	UNIT COST	TOTAL

PAYMENT METHOD:

☐ CHECK
☐ MONEY ORDER
☐ MASTERCARD
☐ VISA

MEMBER DISCOUNT, 20%	$ _____
CA RESIDENTS SALES TAX 8.25%	$ _____
SUBTOTAL	$ _____
POSTAGE 15% UPS: 20% ($2 MIN.)	$ _____
MEMBERSHIP(S)	$ _____
ADDITIONAL CONTRIBUTION	$ _____
TOTAL ENCLOSED	$ _____

_____
NAME ON CARD

_____
CARD NUMBER   EXP. DATE

_____
SIGNATURE

MAKE CHECK OR MONEY ORDER PAYABLE TO:

FOOD FIRST, 398 – 60TH STREET, OAKLAND, CA 94618

FOR GIFT MEMBERSHIPS & MAILINGS, PLEASE SEE COUPON ON REVERSE SIDE

FOOD FIRST GIFT BOOKS

Please send a Gift Book to (order form on reverse side):

NAME _____

ADDRESS _____

CITY/STATE/ZIP _____

FROM _____

FOOD FIRST PUBLICATIONS CATALOGS

Please send a Publications Catalog to:

NAME _____

ADDRESS _____

CITY/STATE/ZIP _____

NAME _____

ADDRESS _____

CITY/STATE/ZIP _____

NAME _____

ADDRESS _____

CITY/STATE/ZIP _____

FOOD FIRST GIFT MEMBERSHIPS

☐ Enclosed is my tax-deductible contribution of:

☐ $35   ☐ $50   ☐ $100   ☐ $1,000   ☐ OTHER

Please send a Food First membership to:

NAME _____

ADDRESS _____

CITY/STATE/ZIP _____

FROM _____